A view of Portsmouth clearly showing Point and the harbour entrance by Hendrick Danckerts. c.1675."Supplied by Royal Collection Trust/© H M Queen Elizabeth II 2012"

A view of Portsmouth Point (part) by Hendrick Danckerts. c. 1675."Supplied by Royal Collection Trust/© H M Queen Elizabeth II 2012"

A view of Portsmouth Point (part) by Hendrick Danckerts. c.1675. "Supplied by Royal Collection Trust/© H M Queen Elizabeth II 2012"

Published by Gower Lloyd

Email: glloyd@ahistoryofpoint.com

Website: www.ahistoryofpoint.com

Copyright © Gower Lloyd, November 2015

ISBN 978-0-9934140-0-8

British Library Cataloguing in Publication Data.

A catalogue record for this book is available from the British Library.

Designed by Gower Lloyd.

Second edition (revised December 2018)

A
History of Point
Portsmouth's Spice Island

Contents

Acknowledgements

The author would like to thank John Stedman and his staff at the Portsmouth History Centre, Central Library, for the assistance given to him whilst undertaking the book research. Thanks also to Katy Ball, Collection Registrar at Portsmouth Museum for providing numerous photos, some of which are reproduced by kind permission of Portsmouth Museums Service, Portsmouth City Council.

In addition, acknowledgements are given to the work of numerous authors of the *Portsmouth Papers*, a wonderful collection of historical information published about Portsmouth.

Thanks are given to my daughter, Nicky, for painstakingly reading my early drafts and providing suggestions to improve and enhance the book and I extend my gratitude to my friend Derek Lines for undertaking a great deal of work in enhancing photos and providing original art work during the preparation of the book.

My appreciation and thanks are extended to Richard Thorne and Keith Feltham and others that helped in the checking of the book text and to Nigel Grundy for his guidance and help in the preparation and editing of the book.

During the time I have been researching this book, many people have allowed me to photograph their pictures and copy their personal records and for this I am extremely grateful. The provenance of some items is unknown, but where the origin is known it is acknowledged beneath the picture. If I am notified of any omissions I will update the picture credits in any further reprinting of this book.

Finally my eternal thanks are given to my long suffering wife, Yvonne, who assisted in proof reading and endured all the time I spent researching and writing the book, and to my father for providing historical information for inclusion in the book, and encouragement during its preparation.

Others, too numerous to mention have also helped me and for their contributions I am truly grateful.

Introduction

Portsmouth Point, part of which was first built on in the fifteenth century is a unique place with a fascinating history. It is known locally as "Spice Island", possibly named so due to all the spices and Eastern goods that passed through it when the East India Company and its large fleet of ships were regular visitors in the seventeenth and eighteenth centuries.

This book attempts to give readers an idea of the colourful place this must have been throughout its history with mariners visiting from all parts of the world. It was visited by crews of both the Royal Navy and Merchant Navy and sailors from many foreign ports and at one time during its history it boasted nearly fifty pubs, together with beer houses, within its small geographical area.

The Point was an island for many years with King James's gate at its entrance and a bridge beyond, putting it outside the town of Portsmouth, which contributed to its reputation for lawlessness and notoriety.

Many of the people who lived here were poor and lived in damp and cramped conditions, where outbreaks of illness were commonplace and Jews and prostitutes were numerous, together with vagabonds and other scoundrels seeking to fleece the sailors of their hard earned wages and sometimes prize money when coming ashore after long voyages.

Vessels, large and small, set off from Point for destinations home and abroad and coaching inns were established to transport people by road to London and beyond.

Maritime trades of all description were in existence to service all the boats and crews that regularly visited the area, and for many years the Press gangs were active on Point often arriving at the Sally Port and then heading to the Point capturing local men and forcing them to serve aboard his Majesty's ships, both home and abroad.

During the smuggling era, the Point would have seen a multitude of goods passing through with so many ship's crews from all around the world landing here.

The Camber which was a very sheltered inlet was a focal point for much trade throughout the years with an incredible diversity of goods arriving to service an expanding population. Coal was a major import and fruit and vegetables were regularly offloaded at the quays and a fishing fleet has always existed here and even today is still active. Moderately sized ships were built and maintained in the Camber area and numerous shipyards existed throughout the centuries, building craft of many designs

The Sally Ports, used by many sailors for coming ashore and later leaving to voyage abroad to fight sea battles, were also used on numerous occasions for the departure of fleets setting off to establish colonies overseas and aid the expansion of the British Empire.

Numerous activities that occurred throughout the centuries on the Point are outlined in the book giving an insight into what life would have been like during that period. Many very famous people have been associated with Point throughout the centuries helping to shape both Britain's history and that of Spice Island.

General Maps of Spice Island

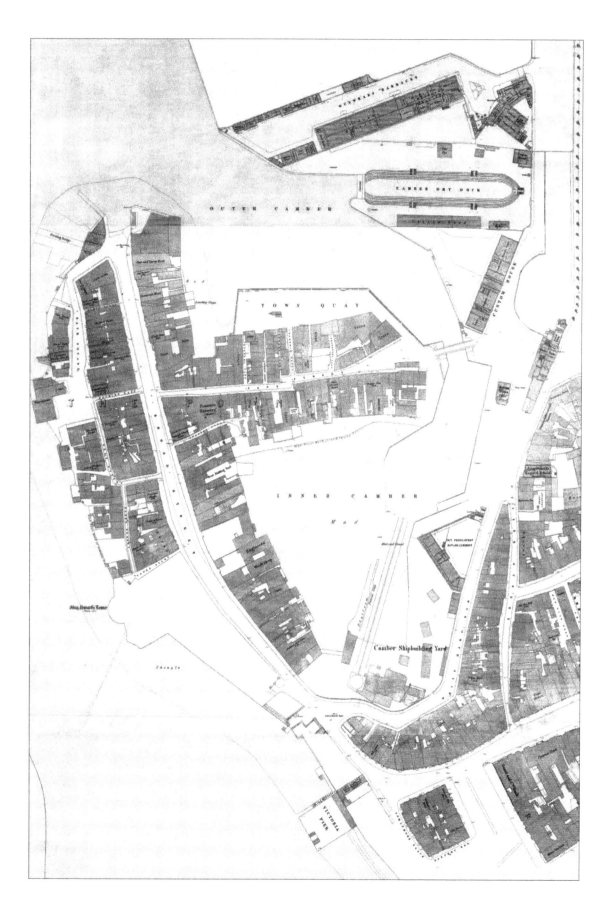

This map of Spice Island is part of an original map that was engraved and published at the Ordnance Survey Office Southampton in 1867, and supplied to the author by the University Library, University of Portsmouth.

It shows the area at that time, including important locations and buildings. However, some buildings and sites referred to in this book were established post 1867 and have been added to the map. The purpose of this master map and the maplets that follow, together with their respective keys, is to provide the reader with an idea of the geography of the area.

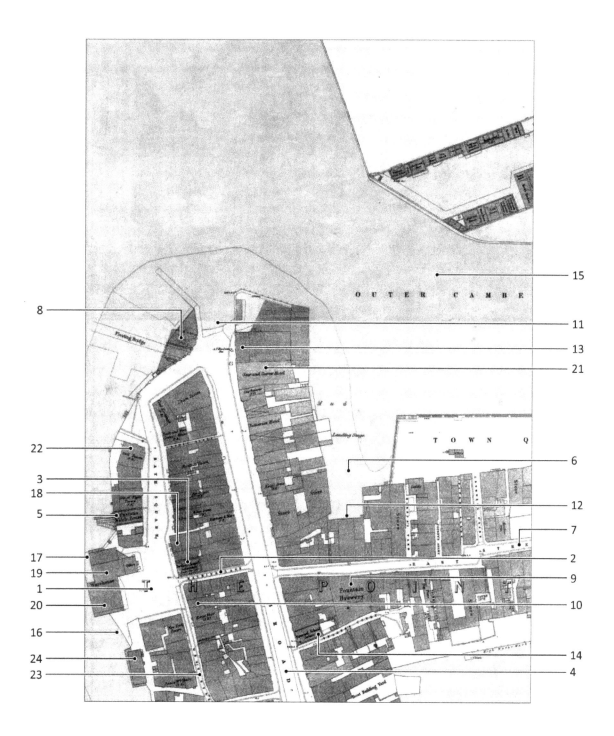

Key

1. Bath Square.
2. Bathing Lane.
3. Bethel Chapel.
4. Broad Street.
5. Customs Watch House.
6. Dirty Corner.
7. East Street.
8. Floating bridge office.
9. Fountain brewery.
10. Harry Feltham's yard.
11. IOW Car ferry slipway (pre 1961).
12. IOW Car ferry slipway (1961)
13. Last house in Portsmouth
14. National School.
15. Outer Camber
16. Pickfords beach.
17. Pickfords quay.
18. Portsmouth Sailing Club.
19. *Quebec Hotel*.
20. Quebec House.
21. *Star & Garter Hotel*.
22. *Still & West*.
23. West Street.
24. Weeke's wharf

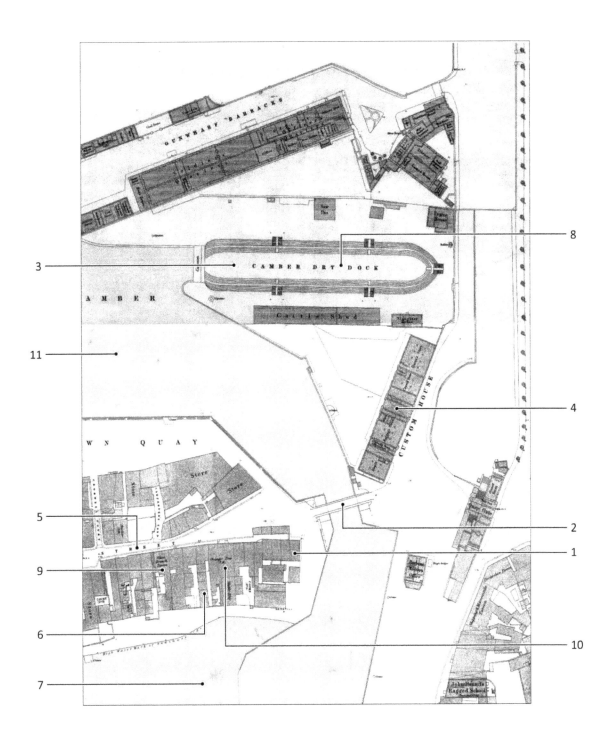

Key

1. *Bridge Tavern*.
2. Camber Bridge.
3. Camber Dry Dock.
4. Customs House (1828).
5. East Street.
6. Fraser & White coal bunker.
7. Inner Camber.
8. IOW Car ferry (existing).
9. *Olive Branch tavern*.
10. *Orange Tree Tavern*.
11. Outer Camber.

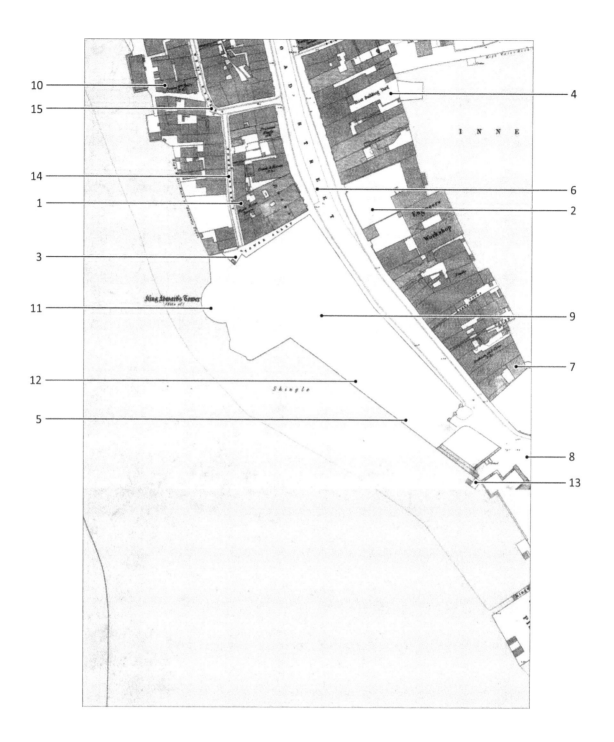

Key

1. *Black Horse Tavern*.
2. *Blue Posts Hotel*.
3. Capstan Square.
4. Clemens boatyard.
5. Eighteen Gun Battery.
6. Fisherman's Row.
7. George Feltham's boatyard.
8. King James's Gate.
9. Point Barracks.
10. *Prince William Henry*.
11. Round Tower.
12. Sally Port
13. Sally Port (original).
14. Tower Street.
15. West Street.

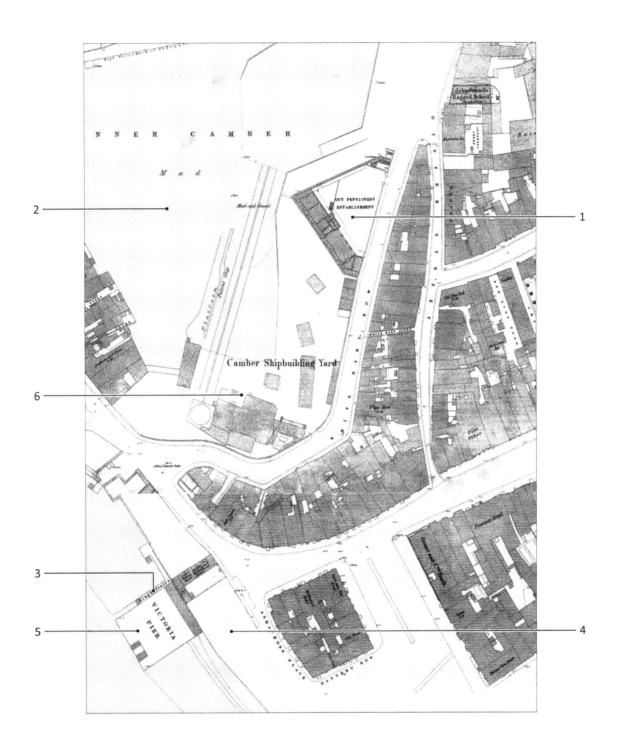

Key

1. Camber Bastion.
4. Square Tower.
2. Inner Camber
5. Victoria pier.
3. Kings stairs
6. Vospers boatyard.

Panoramic Views of Spice Island

This unique panoramic view of Point and Portsmouth town was painted by a veteran of Trafalgar from the roof of the Semaphore Tower in 1825. The artist, Francis Spencer Smyth, Commander R. N. was born in 1791 and joined the navy in 1803, aged 11. He was a midshipman on H.M.S. Defiance at the battle of Trafalgar aged 13, and later was promoted to Admiral in 1878.

These three photos c.1861 by Jebez Hughes show the harbour entrance shoreline in some detail. The floating bridge can clearly be seen in the upper photo berthed on its slipway with H. M. S. Vernon behind. In the middle picture can be seen the *Isle of Wight tavern*, *Quebec Hotel* and the large Pickfords buildings nearby to the south, together with the very dense housing fronting on to the foreshore. In the lower picture the *Black Horse Tavern* is clearly visible, together with Burridge's tower, the fortifications and the Cathedral behind.

A delightful harbour entrance view drawn by W. H. Snape c.1897 showing the Floating Bridge terminal on the left with the Vulcan building in Gunwharf behind, together with the *Still & West, Isle of Wight tavern*, J. D. Felthams's boatyard, HM Customs watch house and the *Quebec Hotel* on the right. *"Illustrated History of Portsmouth"* by W.G.Gates, Reproduced courtesy of The News Portsmouth.

A very old photo, pre 1900, showing part of the Point, with East Street and its properties on the left and a dense cluster of houses bordering Broad Street. The entrance to Haslar creek can clearly be seen, together with part of Gosport town.

Panoramic view of Spice Island painted by M.Snape in 1910. Image courtesy of Neville Churcher.

This photo of the Point slipways c. 1920 clearly shows one of the Gosport passenger ferries berthed alongside. Although most Gosport ferries ran between the Gosport ferry pontoon and the Hard, Portsea, there was also a service between Gosport and Point. The boats that used to operate taking visitors on "round the harbour" trips, berthed nearby. The "Last house in Portsmouth" (102 Broad Street), the *Union tavern, Still & West and Quebec hotel* are clearly visible in the picture.

Pre Second World War photo in which the large Pickfords buildings behind Weeke's wharf can clearly be seen.

Post Second World War photo c.1960 with one of the Power Station's chimneys clearly visible, together with the crane that operated on Pickfords wharf.

A current view (August 2015) with the Land Rover BAR building now clearly dominating the skyline of Spice Island.

Preface

Growing up on Point

"Spice Island" or "Point" in Old Portsmouth is a very special place and from the time it was first inhabited in the early 17th century has been one of the most vibrant and interesting areas of Portsmouth with its rich maritime history.

I spent the first 25 years of my life growing up on the Point and even in the 1950s, 60s and 70s the place was special with so much going on all the time.

I was lucky to have witnessed the end of an era in so many ways as I remember travelling on the old chain ferry (Floating Bridge) across the harbour from the Point to Gosport and recall the Isle of Wight car ferry landing on the slipway at the end of Broad Street and the long queues of traffic in Broad Street waiting to embark on both these vessels.

Traffic queuing in Broad Street for the Floating Bridge to Gosport.

1

The Floating Bridge ceased operations in 1959 and the IOW car ferries later moved into the Camber in 1961 using the purpose built new slipway and terminal adjacent to East street, before moving again to the current berth on the north side of the Camber.

In those days the Camber was a more active place than today with colliers bringing in coal to the Inner Camber and the larger colliers, *Pompey Power* and *Pompey Light* berthing at the old dry dock adjacent to HMS Vernon unloading coal for the now long gone Power Station.

Colliers also discharged their coal by the overhead gantries into the huge Fraser & White silos that were sited near the *Bridge Tavern* where we used to play and often returned home in a filthy state.

The collier *Pompey Power* © Charlie Hill.

HMS Vernon was then still in operation and in its later years always had numerous minesweepers berthed alongside.

During the years I grew up in the area, on a couple of occasions I remember seeing cars that had driven over the edge of the quay but were fortunately saved by landing on boats below. However, one lad we knew who was employed by W. G. Lucas, the sailmaker, was larking around on the quay in his van near the *Bridge Tavern* one day and accidentally drove over the edge. The car's hazard lights were still flashing as it sank, but fortunately he escaped through a window, but he was less fortunate with his job as he was later sacked!

Fortunate soft landing for a car in 1975.

As a youngster I recall the Jersey Royal potatoes being unloaded from the Channel Islands arriving in the Camber in the spring on vessels like the *Princess Wilhelmina* and crawling underneath the lorries as they were loading up, looking for spuds that had fallen out of broken containers and then taking them home to my mother.

Stevedores unloading cauliflowers in the Camber c. 1959. Photo courtesy of Helen Mabel Smith (1905-1990).

I also remember the tomatoes and cabbages arriving and the damage caused to the containers which used to regularly fall off suspiciously whilst being transported. The stevedores used to put them to one side and help themselves later.

My father once told me a story associated with arrival of the Jersey Royals in the Camber, and it was about one of the locals working in the sheds who told my father to come along later one evening when he would give him some free potatoes as he was a friendly chap and liked my father.
Just as he was handing over the potatoes to my father a police car came around the corner with its headlamps on and as the officer got out of the car he was very quick thinking and said to the officers "I have put your potatoes over there". Whether this was true or not my father didn't know but it put them on the spot and with my father as a witness they drove off. Perhaps they came back later!

The stevedores were a happy bunch of men and my friends and I used to play football with them in the sheds when they weren't working. I remember when I was young asking them for donations for fireworks before November 5th as we sat on a street corner with our bonfire guy asking for a "penny for the guy". They were always very generous and good humoured with us.

At that time my friends and I used to collect wood from the local area and helped build the November 5th bonfire at the Point, adjacent to where the Floating Bridge came ashore. It was celebrated much more by communities in those days and many local people came along with their fireworks, as there were no large organised displays then.

One afternoon on November 5th I was in a car being driven across the city and recall seeing numerous unlit bonfires as there were still many old bomb sites around following the Second World War bombing damage.

I used to live next door to one of the local boat builders, Harry Feltham. I remember all the banging and sawing going on in the boat shed throughout the day and seeing the apprentices coming and going and talking to them when they had their lunch as they sat in the public seats on Weeke's wharf. It was a wonderful spectacle seeing the new boats coming out of the shed and being chocked up in Bath Square, prior to launching.

Harry and Stan Feltham, his nephew, built at least one yacht designed by Sparkman and Stephens, the internationally famous American yacht designers and they turned up on one occasion to see the finished yacht and have a trial sail. Apparently Stan refused to allow them to helm the boat on her trials until he had been paid for the work and Sparkman thought this very amusing!

Harry Feltham had a brother named George who was also a very well-known boat builder, and his boat yard backed on to the Inner Camber near Vospers yard in Broad Street.

Harry told my father that when times were hard they often existed eating porridge and he recalls Harry telling him of a trip to Bembridge, Isle of Wight, on one occasion to catch a swan for food.

In addition to the Felthams, there was the commercial ship building operation of Vospers in the Inner Camber. They built smaller warships such as minesweepers and fast patrol boats, some of which were for foreign navies and these could often be seen in the Camber where the marina exists today.

The severe winter of 1963 when the Camber froze over. This photo shows the old Fraser & White concrete silo wall and fishing boats in the foreground, together with the conveyor belts in the background transporting coal from the colliers berthed in the old Dry Dock to the Power Station.

Since many activities in the area were related to boating and yachts, it was not surprising that the well-known sailmaker, W.G Lucas, set up his headquarters and sail loft in Broad Street and was located there for many years.

Although not located on Spice Island, there used to be a business sited near to the "American Bar" on the east side of the Camber called Leekies that sold ex Government goods such as nautical gear, compasses, clocks etc. It was really cheap and an "Aladdin's Cave", was very popular and used by people far and wide searching for bargains.

My recollection of the fishing fleet in the 50s and 60s was of generally smaller boats than today and the moorings were quite haphazard with many boats moored in the middle of the Inner Camber and on the shore behind W. G. Lucas, with other boats moored in "Dirty Corner."

There was a Customs Office located in Bath Square in those days, and sailing vessels from abroad used to regularly come close to their hailing station to request clearance before going into the Camber. I remember doing this myself after sailing back across the Channel from France and sometimes they would turn up in the Camber to clear your yacht and other times would not. After a couple of hours you were free to proceed to your mooring.

Certainly, being brought up on Spice Island at that time provided a great play area with many interesting places to explore and we spent most days playing outside. On one occasion when with a friend we were investigating the uninhabited remains of the famous *Star and Garter*" hotel in Broad Street just prior to its demolition, we were apprehended by a policeman who shepherded us out for our own safety, as it was obviously unsafe. I suppose I must have been aged about 8 years old at the time.

A view of Broad Street at its junction with East Street c.1959 just prior to the demolition of all the premises in the photo on the east side of Broad Street for the construction of the new car ferry terminal.

There was also much sailing activity on Point associated with the Portsmouth Sailing Club and Victory Class, who have both been located on Spice Island for many years and are still there today. The sailing club used to launch their sailing dinghies down their slipway directly into the harbour entrance from their boatyard and during the 1940s and 1950s races were started in the harbour entrance although this later ceased with the increase in commercial traffic.

I remember launching my own boat down this slipway for some years until the slipway fell into disrepair and was eventually abandoned.

Launching then transferred to the Point, or from the Camber slipway, somewhat more sheltered that the old slipway, which could be hazardous in strong onshore winds. With less commercial harbour activity than today the club used to have very active dinghy racing during the week and at weekends, which the "Victory class" still enjoys today.

The Portsmouth Sailing Club headquarters in Bath Square was formerly the office of Arnoldus Louis van den Bergh, shipping agent and consul/vice consul for Belgium, Denmark, Norway, Netherlands, Portugal, Sweden, Turkey and consular agent for Italy and France. The left hand photo above shows the building and the right hand photo shows members boats on Pickfords beach c.1950.

The 1st Portsmouth Sea Scouts were very active in the area keeping some of their boats on Wyllie's beach and having very close ties with the Portsmouth Sailing Club. They were led by their scout leader, Jack Ashdown, an amazing character who was a great instructor and clever man, being expert in all things nautical, in addition to being a brilliant artist, cartoonist and wood carver, having been trained as a shipwright in the Naval Base. The troop is still active today, being based in the large timber building opposite the sailing club in Bath Square which was formerly used by a local rowing club to store their boats. Prior to this it was used for storing fishing nets and may have been used in the nineteenth century for storing and launching boats as the area to the rear of the building was known locally as the "skids".

The sea scouts' boat, *Royal Arthur,* being hauled out of the water at the Point in 1976 with the assistance of sea scouts and members of the Portsmouth Sailing Club.

Point Barracks as it used to be with the high boundary wall
situated on the west side of Broad Street.

In the 1950s and early 1960s the very high wall of Point Barracks still existed in Broad Street making it inaccessible, but as youngsters we used to find our way in there climbing over the fortifications. Today the area is widely open to the public but in those days it was out of bounds and a fascinating place to explore and play games.

In the 1950s before the East street car ferry slipway was built, "Dirty Corner" still existed in the outer Camber where boats were moored and laid up on the foreshore and it was a great place to play and go crabbing and fishing.

"Dirty Corner" with the old timber warehouse in the background. Some boats were on moorings and others dried out on the foreshore c.1958.

Just nearby was the well-known café called Grogan's, where people often used to congregate and I remember visiting here a few times with the Sea Scouts before it was demolished in the late1950s.

Grogan's café prior to its demolition circa 1959

Tidal flooding was a regular event in the area at times of high spring tides and severe weather and it was mainly the residents in Broad Street that suffered. Flood boards slotted in and backed up with clay were a regular sight on these occasions.
The camaraderie was there to see and most residents dealt with these occurrences as part of everyday life. It is hardly surprising that the area regularly flooded, when you consider how many open slipways existed in the area at that time. In this photo a flood board has been put in and sealed up with clay in readiness for flooding c. 1950.

This photo shows Broad Street severely flooded and on occasions like this numerous residents in the street would have had water inside their properties.

The passage of naval vessels in and out of the harbour was a common sight and one often saw new warships heading out for trials, ships returning with paying off pennants and the sad sight of ships being decommissioned, then towed out of the harbour heading for the breaker's yards elsewhere.

Sometimes ships could be seen leaving the harbour towing targets behind them as they headed out into the Channel for target practice by the navy.
There were rare occasions when ships headed off to war at times like the Falklands conflict and other memorable occasions such as the time when the last of our battleships, *HMS Vanguard* went aground nearly hitting the *Still and West* pub as she was being towed off to the breakers yard at the end of her career following decommissioning.

One sight that used to occur regularly in the spring was that of porpoises entering the harbour, but unfortunately this does not happen today. In addition, I recall occasions when nature produced something out of the ordinary, such as the explosion in numbers of harmless "moon" jellyfish, when there were thousands of them, and another occasion when the whitebait were so plentiful that they could be seen being chased into Wyllie's beach by the mackerel and there were thousands washed up on the harbour foreshore.

When my father designed and had his house built on Spice Island in the early 1950s, he was amongst the first to do so after the war and at that time it was not the most fashionable place to live. The area could be a rough place on occasions and I recall him once finding a drunken sailor asleep in the front porch in the morning.

In addition to the ferries operating from Spice Island, boats used to operate from the Point in the summer taking visitors on trips around the harbour. There was the well-known firm of watermen, J Butcher & Sons Ltd, in their blue boats and other smaller independent operators that were also licenced.

J Butchers & Sons Ltd, established in 1809, used to assist with Commercial towage operations as ships arrived and left the harbour and also operated round the harbour trips from their base to the east of Clarence Pier.

In Bath Square next to *Quebec House* was Pickfords wharf, from where Pickfords operated for many years, with ships berthing alongside, particularly from the Isle of Wight.

Pickfords used to leave their trailers and lorries littered around Bath Square and it was a really busy place during the week with trailers and their loads continually being moved.

A typical scene in Bath Square in the 1950s and 1960s when Pickfords were operating.

I recall all the problems my father had with this company which were sited directly opposite our house. This was because their lorries collided with our bay window on many occasions causing much damage whilst manoeuvring in Bath Square.

It was a happy day for us and many other residents when this operation closed down freeing up a lot of parking space in the process.

Bath Square in 1957.

The fortifications near the Sally Port are known locally as the "Hot Walls" by many and it has been documented that the "Hot Walls" were so called because this was where the red hot shot was prepared during the Spithead Mutiny in 1797, although never used and their location may well have been in front of the Saluting Platform or Ten Gun battery to the east.

This area has always been very busy in the summer and it was no different in the 1950s and 1960s when lots of families would regularly visit from Portsea and other parts of the city during the summer holidays. Children would congregate and jump into the sea from the fortifications nearby and swim in the "Bunny", the warm water outfall from the Power Station which in earlier years had been discharged into the Inner Camber then later rerouted along White Hart Road after the Second World War to be discharged into the harbour entrance.

The warm water of the "Bunny" also attracted numerous sea bass and lots of fishermen.

A very busy summer scene at Sally Port.

Jumping off the roof next to the Round Tower into the harbour was seen as some sort of initiation in those days and we all did it, myself included
Looking back now, I certainly wouldn't recommend doing it today as I realise how dangerous this is and large fines have now been imposed to discourage youngsters from doing this.

Swimming across the harbour entrance was another challenge many local boys did, crossing at slack tide when no shipping was about, but this is not possible today, nor recommended, with the very large number of ships entering and leaving the harbour.
We also used to regularly swim from the Point during the summer on a fast ebb tide arriving near the Sally Port beach very quickly and then swimming ashore.

Another activity for some of us youngsters in the 1960s was beachcombing, finding all sorts of things in an area that was a lot more accessible and lucrative at that time. We used to collect old copper and brass fastenings thrown onto the foreshore from local boat builders and in addition we would find coins and other interesting things that had been thrown into the sea from the *Still and West* pub. We also had "Dirty Corner" and the Inner Camber to explore at low tide which was more accessible in those days.

There were also interesting finds to be had on the beaches after strong onshore gales.

The Point and Camber can still become very busy today with the Isle of Wight Car Ferry berthing, the fishing boats landing their catches, and commercial and pleasure craft manoeuvring but it has lost so much of its old character in a relatively short space of time.

Although Point can become very crowded during the summer with the waterside pubs overflowing with people and cars searching out parking spaces, it is so different to bygone days when more of the local residents had established roots in the area and so much more was going on.

During my lifetime much residential development has taken place, replacing many maritime activities that have either closed down or moved elsewhere. This has obviously impacted enormously on the character of the area.

I consider myself very fortunate to have been brought up on the Point in my youth at a time when the area was so much more attractive to a youngster than today.

Chapter 1

The History of Development on Point

"Point" is a natural shingle peninsula sited on the eastern shore at the entrance to Portsmouth harbour surrounded by water on three sides, one of which has a shallow sheltered inlet called the Camber.

The area has always been of strategic importance for the protection of Portsmouth harbour from invasion and for this reason, the first building constructed on this spit was the Round Tower, built in the early fifteenth century to protect the harbour entrance. Shortly afterwards a similar tower was constructed on the opposite side of the harbour in Gosport.

Sometime later in the 16th century a couple of lime kilns and two other buildings were constructed near the Round Tower.

These are clearly shown on the map below, together with the "mighty chaine" that spanned the harbour entrance on occasions of likely invasion by foreign powers.

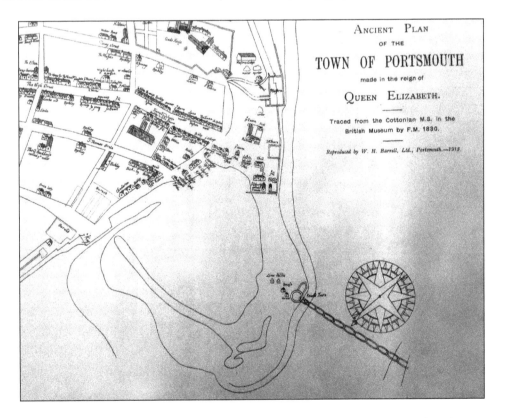

Extract from an ancient plan of the town of Portsmouth made some time in the reign of Queen Elizabeth I (1558-1603) traced from the Cottonian Manuscripts in the British Museum. © of the British Library Board.

Prior to this map, the earliest known plan of Portsmouth (dated some time before 1540) shows the "Pales", (a palisade or picket fence and a gate across the neck of Point) outside the town, thought to have been completed during the fifteenth century. During the reign of Queen Elizabeth, a strong stone wall was constructed across the neck of Point, replacing the Pales with a strong gate known as Poynt Gate. This gate was located at the site where King James's Gate was later built in 1687 in order to control access in and out of Point via a bridge across a moat, meaning that at high water Point was effectively an island.

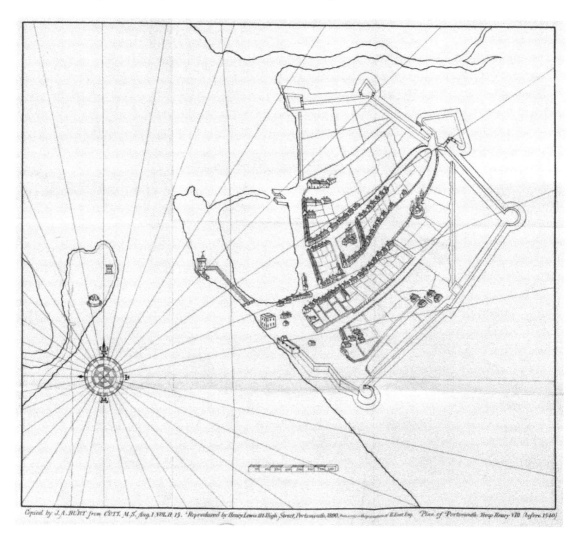

The earliest known plan of Portsmouth clearly showing "the Pales" and gate on the Point. (Date before 1540). © of The British Library Board.

The historical association between Point and the production, consumption and exportation of alcohol goes back a long way: it is thought that the first house built on the Point was a drink shop and early maps also show a number of brewing houses probably constructed in the late sixteenth/early seventeenth century.

Storehouses were built on the Camber quay to store beer produced by the local brewery in the early sixteenth century, and the *Cowdray* painting of 1545 shows men shifting casks from stores to ships, the crane wharf near "the store broomhowses," and the *Swanne* bake house (1544) just inside the Point Gate. One of the earliest Portsmouth maps in existence (c.1545) shows buildings lining the eastern Camber shore, with a cluster inside Point Gate. [1]

Although Spice Island was almost uninhabited in the sixteenth century it was largely built up by the 1670s. In the 1590s waste ground was used for the construction of storehouses for merchants and military personnel and in the early seventeenth century tenements were built on substantial plots by a cordwainer, sailor, gunner and shipwright, while by 1610 four inns had appeared along Broad Street. The peninsula around Smocke Alley (East Street) started to become frequented with seamen and fishermen in the early seventeenth century and the allocation of grants of beach ground marked the colonisation of the southern shoreline. [1]

The map below, drawn by De Gomme in 1668, shows Broad Street as we know it today but named as High Street and soon other roads were constructed off Broad Street, including Smocke Alley (East Street), Cubbs Alley (Tower Street), West Street, Bathing House Square, Bathing Lane and numerous other courts and alleys where dense housing had built up. Some of these courts were closed at both ends and approached by covered passages, and in them the filth flooding from privies and the refuse discarded by the inhabitants accumulated. In some courts there was only one tap and a single privy pot served 60 people. [2]

Many of the inhabitants of Point were very poor and living conditions were very unhealthy with open sewers in the streets, livestock roaming free, and a lack of fresh water that resulted in diseases being rife, some often fatal to infants. It is hardly surprising that diseases like the Plague spread very fast in densely populated areas like the Point with the poor standards of living accommodation and sanitation.

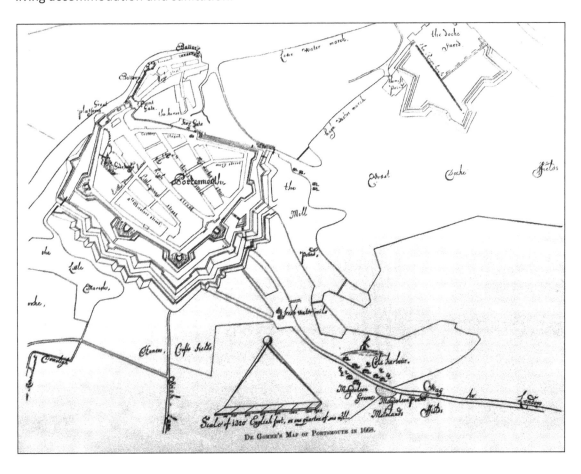

Part of De Gomme's map of Portsmouth 1668. © of the British Library Board.

15

The Camber continued to flourish; a ship building industry began to be established, and businesses developed to provide services and trade with the Royal Navy, Merchant Navy, East India Company and foreign vessels.

However, the Camber was never able to really fulfil its potential, as its expansion was stifled by the navy, which had its own shipbuilding services provided by an ever expanding larger naval Dockyard.

In the first half of the eighteenth century the population increased at Point and properties were built on Point and alongside "Dirty Corner" in the Camber, extending out into the sea.

The earliest surviving Poor Rate Book of 1730 lists 150 rateable properties on Point, many probably storehouses. [1]

Tidal flooding has always been a problem on Point and has occurred regularly throughout the years on occasions when spring tides coincided with very strong winds from the southerly quarter and low pressure weather systems. This would have made living conditions in basements and cellars dreadful and would have added to the pollution of any fresh water systems in existence.

In *The Borough*, published by Robert Wilkins in 1748, a description of Portsmouth is included, part of which describes the scarcity of water as follows:

> In 1748 Point was badly supplied with water and that which was available was saline and this was so scarce that if it were not for the showers of rain, which were caught by everybody, the people could not exist. It would appear they were content to follow their forefathers' example to pay, one house with another, forty shillings per annum for the delivery of a fresh water supply by travelling water carts.

"William Gilpin, noted for his tours of picturesque locations across Britain in the late eighteenth century, observed, when visiting Portsmouth in 1774, that:

> One of the great deficiencies of Portsmouth is the want of water. There are springs in different parts of the harbour but not being collected into a head, they are inconvenient. The garrison is particularly ill supplied. This set an adventurous tradesman who lived on Point, as it is called, to dig near his house in quest of water.
> At a depth of sixty feet he found a muddy bottom and dug up an antique anchor, but no water appeared, so he still went on. At the depth of twenty feet more he came to sand and found symptoms of water, but instead of digging farther he tried an experiment. He bored a large pile and drove it deep into the sandy stratum that he had found. As soon as the pile touched the main spring, the water gushed so plentifully through it, and even to fill the well to the brim and to run over.
> This, however was only the first ebullition of the water. It soon sank but continued to stand at a height of eight or nine feet from the surface which gave a depth of seventy feet of good water in the well.

The observation by Gilpin was not an isolated incident, since inhabitants of Point tried to extract water on a private basis by sinking wells, but the water often became polluted by neighbours and passers-by. However, by the late eighteenth century there were public wells or pumps in all the main streets of Portsmouth. [3]. On 30th June 1788 it was reported that three more wells were to be sunk in Broad Street and pumps erected in them. [11]

The Point was plagued by poor sanitation and the shortage of privies meant that chamber pots were emptied into the cowls or passages, or into the Camber where they accumulated.

It is reported that at one time in the mid nineteenth century about thirty pigs were kept in a confined space behind a dwelling house in East Street, with the dung being deposited in an open yard which must have created an intolerable stench.

It is claimed that the fortifications were partly responsible for the Point's deficient ventilation and absence of a full water supply or drains, as they interfered with the natural drainage.

Eventually, local laws were introduced on Point to try to improve the quality of life. Likewise fines were imposed for crimes of antisocial behaviour that included the following :- "Persons not cleansing the Camber gutter before their houses"; "Persons emptying domestic slops out of their window"; "For opening shoppe windows selling food and wares on the Sabbath"; "Any person shooting wild fowl or geese at or near the Round Tower"; "Sunday waggon driving was stopped and a fine was put upon Butchers who sold veal not three weeks old, and for those who threw dead fish into the Camber"; "The Chamberlain was warned to make up a "sufficient cage" and a "cucking stool" for ducking female scolds in the Point Camber". [4]

Point developed very fast during the seventeenth and eighteenth centuries and was noted throughout the world for its numerous pubs, taverns and hotels and its other attractions. Indeed, by 1716 nearly half of the entire refreshment houses (public houses, brandy shops and coffee houses) in the old town were on Point.

Sailors knew that when their ships returned to anchor in Spithead after a voyage abroad, they would be taken ashore to the Point to enjoy its hospitality, which included the opportunity to visit brothels and gambling dens and to indulge in other such vices. It was a place where sharp practices prevailed and sailors were often the victims, losing all their hard earned wages or prize money during the course of just a few days.

Caricature by Thomas Tegg 1811 © National Maritime Museum, Greenwich, London which shows Jack penniless after his run ashore.

Being "outside" the town, Point enjoyed many privileges including the right for licensed victuallers to keep their businesses open practically day and night, and for years this part of town was a nightly scene of Bacchanalian orgies. [5]

In 1729 Point was described as the Wapping of Portsmouth and some have compared it to Port Royal in Jamaica founded in 1518. Port Royal was home to English and Dutch sponsored privateers and other pirates from around the world during the latter half of the seventeenth century. It was notorious for its gaudy displays, wealth and loose morals, and most residents were pirates, cutthroats or prostitutes. It was destroyed by an earthquake, tsunami and fire in 1692.

In the eighteenth and nineteenth centuries it was not unusual to see press gangs operating on Point, as they would often come ashore at the Sally Port and then head onto Point effectively trapping their prey. It was a cruel and very unpopular practice which was compared to white slavery and it was a happy day for many when it was abolished sometime in the 19th century.

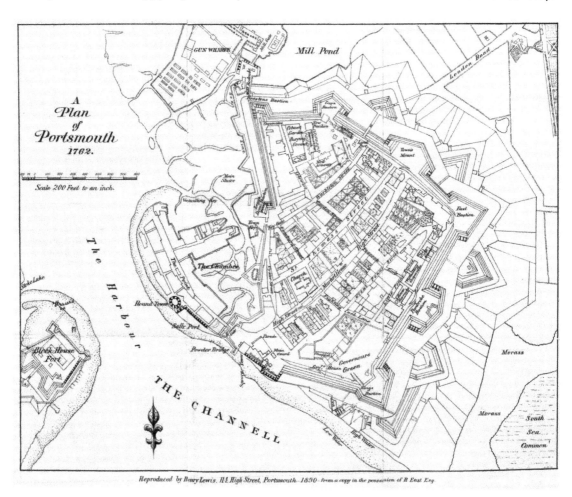

Plan of Portsmouth 1762. © of the British Library Board.

Typical businesses that are listed in Portsmouth Directories in the late eighteenth/early nineteenth century on Point included sail makers, ship's chandlers, slop sellers, watch makers, coppersmiths, silversmiths, shipwrights, rope makers, coopers and coal merchants, together with the usual day to day shops and trades that one would expect.

A beautifully detailed drawing of a greengrocer's shop on Portsmouth Point in 1774 by
Gabriel Bray. © National Maritime Museum, Greenwich, London.

In 1785 a Customs House was built near the bottom of Broad Street and according to an 1817
report it had many staff including one Collector, one Comptroller, 8 Clerks, 2 Surveyors, 4
Landing waiters, 1 Searcher, 3 Coast waiters, 2 Tide surveyors, 2 Warehouse keepers, 6 Lockers
and 50 Tide waiters, together with numerous part time staff. This was a very large workforce
and they had to ensure all the relevant taxes and duties were paid on goods as well as dealing
with the perpetual problem of smuggling.

In 1798 the imports of this Customs House were £79,000, coast duties £15,500 and exports
£2,000. The duties on wine alone were £22,000, which increased in the year 1815 to the large
amount of £137,912! [6]   The sums today would equate to £millions.
Prior to this the Customs revenue was reported as being £3,900 in 1710 increasing to £11,600
in 1760.
In the late 18th century a staggering 15 million eggs were imported from France paying a duty
of £5,300.

The Naval Post Office for the delivery and receipt of letters for both Merchants and King's ships
was located near the lower end of Broad Street, and in 1754 a Bathing House was built in Bath
Square, adjoining the Quebec Hotel.

An eloquent description of Point is included in Motley's *History of Portsmouth*, 1801:

> A place equally known and celebrated for its eccentricities in all parts of the world, where the
> navy or commerce of Great Britain has left or retains any vestiges. This street is divided from
> Portsmouth by a draw-bridge at that part of the fortifications called the Old Sally Port. This
> street is filled with one of the most heterogeneous assemblages of traffic and conviviality that is
> perhaps to be found in the same extent in any one street, and in any one part of the world.
> Liquor shops, contract taverns, Jew shopmen, tailors and drapers jostle Christian pawnbrokers,
> watch jobbers and trinket merchants; cook-shops, eating houses, and ordinaries vie with each
> other to entertain all classes, from the guests of the cabin to those of the forecastle, and whilst
> honest and hearty Jack is dancing with his favourite girl in the lower decks of a liquor shop, his

respectable superiors are enjoying aloft, in the rooms of a tavern, the fruits of their bravery, in that style of elegance their distinguished talents and characters so eminently merit.

William Burridge built the Baltic Wharf in 1808 and later a tower in the Inner Camber with a lookout; this was a major landmark on Point but unfortunately the tower, known locally as Burridge's Folly, burnt down in 1865. In 1842, due to the expansion of Portsea and Landport in Portsmouth town, a swing bridge was erected across the Camber providing another means of access to Point from the town.

Coaching inns grew up in the area as Portsmouth expanded. On Point, the *Blue Posts Hotel* in Broad Street, was a particularly well-known coaching house, providing regular coach services to and from London and other places in the country. Other pubs and hotels also provided these services to some degree but were not as famous, well established, or as large as the *Blue Posts*. In addition to travel by coach, travel by sea was expanding during the eighteenth and nineteenth centuries and vessels could be booked at numerous establishments, mainly pubs and hotels, on Point. Transport was available within the harbour, to the Isle of Wight and to various ports along the coast.

There were also regular voyages to and from France, and the *Quebec Hotel* in Bath Square, in addition to providing a regular service to Ryde on the Isle of Wight and Havre, also organised voyages for people wishing to go to India and other parts of the world.

However, with the introduction of the railways, coach travel diminished and Portsmouth residents caught these trains at the stations in the town rather than on Point. Furthermore, Point also became less of a focal point for steam boat travel in the late nineteenth century as fewer vessels called in or started their voyages from here.

During the eighteenth and nineteenth century the local wherrymen based in Gosport and at Point plied their trade ferrying people throughout the harbour, to the Isle of Wight and to and from the Men of War that lay at anchor in Spithead and in the harbour.
The trips to naval ships at Spithead were often made by Jewish pedlars and prostitutes plying their trade in order to coerce sailors to part with their money.

Point produced many maritime pilots in the last part of the nineteenth century and they were among the most successful along the English Channel, and when first class certified men retired from the Navy, they generally settled down as Point pilots. [4]

The Association for Piloting ships was established at Trinity House, London, and the brethren had the power of examining, licensing and regulating pilots, who fell into the categories of ordinary, first class, choice, river and sea going members. It was a very lucrative calling, with its importance increasing with the progress of ship building to meet the expansion of commerce.

Pilots working for the Peninsular & Orient Company for example, were said to earn from £1000 to £1500 per annum in the nineteenth century.

In the late eighteenth century Portsmouth's harbour was described by William Gilpin as being large enough to contain all the shipping in Europe. He wrote:

> Besides innumerable skiffs and smaller vessels plying about this ample basin, we counted between 50 and 60 sail of the line. Some of these were unrigged and some in commission with their colours flying.

He describes the harbour entrance as being 300 yards across and ships of war of the third and fourth rates can access after any state of tide and the largest men of war at half-tide.

The ships anchored in the harbour are so well protected that a first-rater has very little motion at anchor, even in conditions of strong winds and fast flowing tides.

> The fleets of England ride in safety at Spithead which is a natural deep water anchorage and stretches 5 or 6 leagues and is well secured from every wind by the Isle of Wight till they are reinforced by the several ships intended to join them, and each is equipped and leaves the harbour. [7]

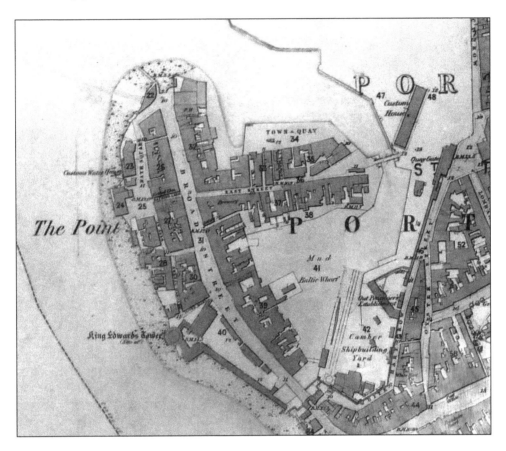

Map of Point 1868. © Crown Copyright reproduced from 1868 Ordnance Survey Map.

Living standards had begun to improve by the end of the eighteenth century. By the late 1700s the streets had been paved and rubbish disposal organised.
Arrangements had also been put in place for the drains and gutters to be flushed and public wells and pumps kept in order. [76]
In the mid nineteenth century the death rate of children under five was over 8%, while 20% did not live beyond their first year. The cooking facilities were primitive and there was a lack of proper food and clothing, resulting in children developing diseases such and tuberculosis and rickets. [2]

In the Victorian period, night wagons were used at Point to cleanse some of the pits and cess pools and in warm weather the smell was dreadful and coupled with the stench from the nearby moats and the Camber, together with a lack of drainage, it must have been disgusting. In the 1820s gas lighting replaced the old oil lamps, but it was reported in 1841 that Portsmouth was one of a few towns in England which are thus neglected where the drains are not covered as in most towns, nor cleaned by a running stream but are in a foul and stagnant condition. [8]
In 1847 the Point Barracks were constructed on the west side of Broad street, resulting in the loss of 19 properties, at least 8 of which were pubs, demolished to make way for the barracks.

King James's Gate and bridge were demolished circa 1860 to allow free traffic into the area, and trams and later trolley buses were introduced.

Education was very limited on Point before the beginning of the 19th century and many of the poorest children received no schooling, or if they were fortunate, attended one of the few charity schools or a Sunday school. For those slightly better off and able to pay a small fee, elementary schooling was available in Portsmouth from 1812. It is interesting to note the description of the two schools on Point from the Public Health report dated 1851 undertaken by Henry Slight, Physician:

> The Royal Victoria School was an independent school established in Bath Square in 1825 and was known as the Seamen and Marines Children's school.
> There were 60 boys in a room at the top of the Bethel Chapel in Bath Square while the same number of girls were in a room half the size. Henry Slight, after visiting, described the school. "Good situation facing the sea, schoolrooms on 2 floors, both small, badly ventilated. No playground, no urinal or privy for the boys and the girls had a very offensive closet opening out on to the street, and the pit was constantly flushed by the tide. The children played together in the Square but there were complaints about the most offensive disturbance to the neighbourhood."

One of the most famous people to have been educated at the Royal Victoria School was Israel Harding V.C. who was born in 1833 and lived locally in White Hart Row.
He served in the Royal Navy, and the following report was published in the London Gazette on 15th September 1882 describing the circumstances of the award of the Victoria Cross to Mr Israel Harding, Gunner, of Her Majesty's Ship *Alexandra*.
The citation for the Act of Bravery read:

> At about nine o'clock, on the morning of the 11th July 1882, whilst her Majesty's Ship *Alexandra* was engaging the Forts at Alexandria, a 10-inch spherical shell passed through the ship's side and lodged in the main deck. Mr Harding, hearing the shout "there is a live shell just above the hatchway" rushed up the ladder from below, and, observing that the fuse was burning, took some water from a tub standing near, and threw it over the projectile, then picked up the shell and put it into the tub. Had the shell burst, it would probably have destroyed many lives.

Israel Harding V. C. died in 1917 and is buried in Highland Road cemetery, Portsmouth.

Israel Harding.

Headstone in Highland Road cemetery.

The Portsmouth Anglican Infant School, built in 1846 in Broad Street was in a most unwholesome situation, close to the slaughter house, the refuse of which passed on two sides of the school. It was a brick and stone building with a large Elizabethan window in the front and three smaller windows on one side, the doorway being on the other side. There was no playground and the privy was in the yard, 13 feet from the school. The ventilation in the building was good but the surrounding environment was not healthy. The school had 90 pupils on average and was supported by subscription and weekly payments from the children of 1d each.

The school suffered severely in the cholera plague in the mid nineteenth century, and was always affected by epidemics – twelve or fourteen pupils being absent weekly.

The Infants school in Broad Street, originally called the Portsmouth
Anglican Infants School. C.1938. Photo courtesy of Dennis Davis.

Some years later, after the closure of these two schools, children from Point used to go to the Portsmouth Town School located in Gunwharf Road next to the Power Station, often travelling across the Camber Bridge to get there until the bridge closed in 1924.

Point was well known for its fish market in the nineteenth/twentieth century which operated in Bath Square outside the *Still & West* pub, often starting very early in the morning with the catches being landed nearby. Bath Square was very well represented with the fish traders and a glance at a *Portsmouth Directory* dated 1900 shows no less than six fish salesmen living in Bath Square at that time.

Towards the end of the nineteenth century and into the early twentieth century, Point began to decline from its earlier peak as a result of fewer maritime visitors, which lead to the gradual demise of its pubs and some of its businesses as more modernisation occurred.

A "Floating Bridge" chain ferry was introduced between Point and Gosport in 1840 which was very successful for many years, carrying foot passengers, carriages, carts and military traffic before closing down in the late 1950s. Car ferries to the Isle of Wight started from Point in the early twentieth century, first travelling from the beach on the Point, then from a new slipway adjacent to East street, and finally from the current berth on the east side of the Camber. Livestock was transported before this time by towboat operations, starting c. 1825.

In the first half of the twentieth century it was quite normal to see two long queues of traffic in Broad Street waiting to board either the "Floating Bridge" or car ferry to the Isle of Wight.

In addition to lines of traffic, it was not uncommon to regularly see cattle, sheep and pigs being herded along Broad Street from the ferry towards East Street where pens were erected to corral the animals. They were held here for a while before being taken to the slaughterhouse located on the east side of the Camber.

Pigs being corralled in East Street near its junction with Broad Street
c. 1938. Photo courtesy of Dennis Davis.

In the early twentieth century the way of life was changing on Point with the main activities centred on the Camber, which was regularly visited by large colliers to service the Power Station.

There was a seasonal trade in fruit and vegetables, an active fishing fleet and expanding boat building activities, particularly with the arrival of Vosper & Co's yard in the late nineteenth century which became increasingly active with government contracts for building fast patrol boats for the Royal Navy and also for foreign navies.

Point, itself, was also changing, as much of the very old poor quality housing was being demolished, some after being declared unfit for human habitation, for new projects around the Camber.
Furthermore, numerous properties were lost as a result of bombing raids in the Second World War.

During the 20th century Bath Square was often very busy with Pickfords operating there transporting goods to many locations in the country, but with a particular emphasis on trade to and from the Isle of Wight.

W.F Smith, General Carrier's horse drawn trailer outside *Quebec House* in 1906. The container of settler's effects refers to British Columbia, Canada.

Pickfords transport which started trade in Portsmouth in the mid-nineteenth century had a wharf located in Bath Square, sited adjacent to *Quebec House.* It carried out a vibrant trade with the Isle of Wight during the twentieth century, with ships regularly berthing alongside the wharf loading and unloading goods, cattle and other commercial trade including beer.

Pickfords wharf in 1912.

Later British Road Services took over and operated from the site until the 1970s, often filling Bath Square with their trailers.

The Portsmouth Sailing Club members and the 1st Portsmouth sea scouts were often seen on Point and were involved in maritime activities throughout the twentieth century. W.L. Wyllie, the famous marine artist, founded the sea scouts c.1910 and was one of the original founders of the Portsmouth Sailing Club in 1920, which still operates from the same building in Bath Square today.

A major change to the landscape occurred in Broad Street in 1959/1960 when the remaining historic properties on the east side between East Street and Point were demolished to allow the new Isle of Wight car ferry terminal and slipway to be built. Properties that were demolished included the famous old *Star & Garter* Hotel and the "The Last House in Portsmouth".

The Last house in Portsmouth (102 Broad Street) was so named as it was sited at the northern end of Broad Street overlooking the mouth of the Camber.

The house had a colourful history being built in 1656 on beach ground as a wharf and two storehouses. It was leased to his Majesty's Ordnance in 1676 and was then briefly used as the Customs House, before being purchased by an agent of the East India Company (Andrew Lindegren), who was their agent between 1788 and 1815. It later became the premises of the Port of Portsmouth and Ryde United Steam Packet Company in 1865 and then in 1881 it was taken over by the Joint Railway Company who subsequently operated the Isle of Wight car ferries from here. [41]

There is much less activity today on Point, although tourists and visitors flock to the area in the summer months, many visiting the three remaining pubs. There is still a fishing fleet with two large fish retailers, and a small marina exists in the Inner camber. On the town quay there are dry stack facilities for ribs and small speed boats and some ancillary marine businesses.

The most significant event to occur recently was the demolition of the remaining industrial sheds on the Town Quay in 2014, and a successful planning application followed for the construction of a very large purpose-built America's Cup facility by Land Rover BAR, with the intention of winning the America's Cup for Britain.

This cup, first raced for in 1851 over a course around the Isle of Wight, was won and then retained by the Americans for many years until it was won many years later by Australia and subsequently other nations, but Great Britain has never managed to win this very prestigious yacht racing trophy, even though numerous attempts have been made to win it. In sports terms this race is equivalent to the Formula One of yacht racing.

This facility was completed in 2015 with the intention of providing a base to mount a successful campaign to win the America's Cup for Great Britain, hopefully in 2017.
Should this campaign be successful, the City of Portsmouth and its population will be major benefactors and it will add a new chapter to the colourful history of Point.

Chapter 2

Fortifications

Portsmouth was plundered by the French several times in the late fourteenth century due to its inadequate defences. The first defences were erected to the town's boundaries with simple earth and timber ramparts surrounded by a ditch with wood or stone towers at the corners.

However, there were no defences protecting the harbour entrance, until in 1417 during the reign of Henry V, the construction of Portsmouth's first permanent defences was started in the form of the Round Tower, which is thought to have been completed by c.1426. [5]

The Round Tower

William Gates states that in 1420 £50 was expended on the Round Tower, in May 1421 £3,500 was provided and between 1423 and 1426 £690 was expended, although part of this sum was for other works in the town.

It was conceived as one of two towers, one on each side of the harbour entrance with a chain boom stretched between them. The Gosport tower construction began in 1431.

They were built so that "the safe custody of the King's ships may be assured" However, by 1526 the town's defences were said to be in sore ruin and decay and humiliation was once more at Portsmouth's door when in 1538 four French ships pursued a vessel from Southampton, with the unfortunate victim grounding besides Palshyds Bulwarks (near Lumps Fort). The ordnance of the town, being out of order at the time, could offer no assistance and the daring Frenchmen boarded and carried off their prize unresisted after the crew had deserted. [9]

The Gosport tower was of wooden construction and was erected considerably later than the Round Tower. It was already old and outmoded when it was inspected by King Edward VI in 1552 and the visit was reported as follows:

> The King took a bote and went to the wodden toure. Upon viewing of wich, things ther was devised two fortes to be made upon the entry of the haven: one where Ridlei's toure standeth, upon the neke that maketh the Camber, the other upon a like necke, standing upon tother side of the haven, where stode an old bulwarke of wode. This was devised for the strength of the haven. It was ment that, that to the toune side should be both stronger and larger. [10]

The Round Tower was called Master Ridley's Tower, named after John Ridley, Page of the King's long bows, and appointed "Keeper of the Tower and houses called '*Le Blokehouse'and 'Berehouse*'" in 1536.

On the south side of the Round Tower was a small projection called the Murder House, which most probably gave flanking fire to the beach. It appears to have been an early form of caponier and the name "murder" most likely deriving from an early type of gun called a "murderer".

The tower has constantly been at risk from undermining by the sea and in the fifteenth century the town laid down the following regulation:

> Which hathe contynued the space of ij hundrethe yeares and"ore", "that all the passage botes that sayle usithe betwene the yle of wighte and portsmouthe should brynge everye of them once in the yeare one bote lode of rocke stones and leye them within the pyles of the round Tower near to the haven's mouthe by the maiors appointment and order. [11]

The intention of this regulation was to try and build up the sea defences to the tower to prevent undermining, and those that failed to abide by this regulation were ordered to pay a "peace" for every such default, to contribute to the better preservation of the tower.

In the troubled reign of Queen Elizabeth much work was carried out to the fortifications, as the ravishes of time necessitated repairs, for it was said in 1561 the wooden platform of the Round Tower was so rotten that it was feared it would not bear the weight of ordnance (the Round Tower was at that time a tower with wooden floors and roof).

In 1585 it was suggested that the height of the tower should be reduced by one half or more "...as to have consideration for the foundation of the stonework next to the sea syde"

The Round Tower is a Tudor construction to the first stringer and it is likely that the tower was largely reconstructed in Elizabeth's reign, producing six gun ports, three of them now filled, which exist today.

The last works, undertaken during the Napoleonic era involved raising the tower a further 6 feet to its present height and constructing a bomb proof magazine on the top north side of the tower.

Sketch by John Christian Schelky in 1814 showing the works in progress during the Napoleonic period when the tower was extended in height with the addition of the central column and brick vaulting to support the weight of the guns on the roof. The sally port in Eighteen gun battery can clearly be seen on the right of the picture. © National Maritime Museum, Greenwich, London.

The Round Tower, with Burridge's Tower and the Semaphore Tower in the picture. c.1830. © of the British Library Board.

The Mightie chaine of yron.

Portsmouth harbour, being a very important Naval Base, was always vulnerable to foreign invasion, particularly at times of war and because of the relatively short distance between Point and Gosport on the other shore, a novel ingenious defensive strategy was adopted.

Over a long period of time several successive chains were laid across the harbour entrance with the intention that they could be raised by means of capstans and floats to close the harbour entrance.

Known as the"mightie chaine of Yron", a chain was forged with very large links to be stretched across the harbour entrance.

In about 1420 a great iron ring was affixed to the Round Tower for securing such a chain and in 1492 there was a payment for "a chene overthwart the haven" which was later removed circa 1513 and a new one made in 1522. [12]

When John Leland, an English poet and antiquary described as "the father of English local history and bibliography," visited Portsmouth making notes about the town and its fortifications, he commented about there being a mighty chain of yren to draw from tourre to towre" and reported its manufacture and cost in 1522 as being £40. [10]

The first mention of the chain is in a navy account presented in February 1522 by Sir W Fitzwilliam [5]:-

For making the chains to be drawn over Portsmouth Haven.   £40. 0.   0

Hire of boats bearing the chains from 12th June to 31st Jan   £21. 9.   0
at 8d the ton a month.

Henry Slight's *History of Portsmouth* refers to an entry entitled "Portsmouth in 1546" which says:
> There is at this point of the haven of Portsmouth Town a great round Tower almost double in quantity and strength to that on the west side of the haven right again it: and here is a mighty chaine of iron to draw from tower to tower.

However, in the engraving of the sinking of the Mary Rose, a year before, in 1545 no chain is shown, but a windlass is shown on Portsmouth Point, which suggests that the chain and lighters were not ready for deployment at that time..

On a map dated 1565 a chain is shown stretching from the Round Tower to Blockhouse, then known as Monsil's Poynte. The next reference is in George Goring's (Governor of Portsmouth) letter dated 1642 wherein he suggests:

> "there should be a chain to go across it, as had formerly been there"

Although another map c.1584 shows a chain, records suggest it was taken into store in 1585 and later, at the beginning of 1642, Charles 1's Governor requested a chain to go across the harbour mouth as had formerly been there. [12]

On Dec 7th 1664, the following letter was written by John Tippets, a master shipwright:

> These are too certifie that Edward Silvester, of Gosporte, smythe, has given securitie for the making and laying of one substantial chaine for His Majesty's Service at Portsmouth.

Silvester received two payments of £100 for his work.

This chain was to be 260 fathoms in length and documents relating to this chain show it was primarily a mooring chain. The work was delayed by the plague, which raged in both Gosport and Portsmouth at this time, and the failure of the Admiralty to pay for it. The length of chain was subsequently reduced to 175 fathoms and it was finished but not assembled in 1671/72. [12]

Before it was completely fabricated, part of the chain was used somehow across the harbour entrance as a defence against a marauding Dutch fleet in 1667.

On September 25th, 1684, Sir John Steventon wrote to the Commissioners of the navy:
> The lowermost next the yard is from clew to clew 224 fathoms, the middle most 157 fathoms, and the uppermost at the Lake's mouth, 122 fathoms; but there must be some allowance for the bite of the cheynes to hang down.

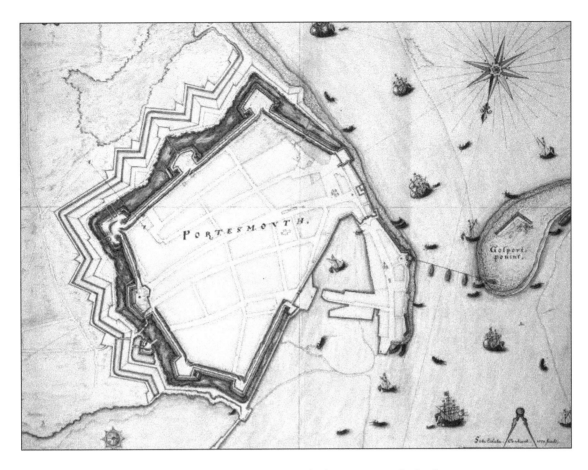

Seventeenth century map clearly showing the boom across the harbour entrance.

In 1707/08 Admiral Sir George Byng wrote whilst in Portsmouth:

> At present there is no boom fixed to lay athwart the harbour's mouth; there was formerly a boom made, which I understand for these 15 years last past has lain neglected, and at best was such, I am told, as would not last four tides in the manner it was fixed, being only pieces of masts linked together with iron fixed thereto, through which a cable was to be reeved, and so laid across the harbour's mouth with chains at each end to prevent its being suddenly cut; however, I have ordered a survey to be had on that boom with the crabbe (capstan?) that is to heave tort the cable, and the chain to be cleared, which now lies under many tons of beach; if there be any apprehension of the enemy's attempts this way, I think that a boom should be put in order. [12]

The Admiral also suggested that that block ships could be deployed for sinking outside the Harbour entrance if necessary.

On February 19th 1744 the following article appeared in the local newspaper:

> There was yesterday advice by one of our Coasters that the French Fleet was within three leagues of the Isle of Wight. All our inhabitants are ordered to take arms at an hour's warning; our chains across the harbour are now getting up and all our Forts are manned and all the guns shotted. We are all in posture of defence and in very high spirits; and we judge as the wind now blows hard they cannot possibly get off our coast and are ready prepared to give them a warm reception if the monsieurs dare to favour us with a visit.

Various drawings and maps during the period from the late seventeenth century until the late eighteenth century show parts of the chain, and records indicate some sort of boom was used to protect the harbour in 1779 in readiness for a Franco-Spanish invasion fleet. However, shortly after this a high ranking official questioned the success of deploying a chain as so many booms had been "forced" elsewhere.

In 1801, Mottley in his *Portsmouth guide* said:

> "The enemy can be stopped by a chain that always lies at the bottom ready to be immediately raised and fastened on both sides"

It was recorded that a chain was forged by Henry Cort in Gosport in 1785 and was in a position on the seabed for use in 1801 and this is probably the chain Mottley referred to.

A Dr Quarrier wrote in the *Portsmouth Standard* in 1842:

> "I recollect the time when a chain was tried from Capstan Square to Blockhouse Point".

It is believed that Dr Quarrier served in the *Royal William* from the autumn of 1799 to the early part of 1801, and it is thought probable that the last chain of which there is any mention was laid down some time in 1801, when the fear of French invasion was rampant and may have been tested at about that time.

The life of one of these chains was a little over 100 years due to the corrosive action of salt water and when not in use the chain lay on the bottom of the harbour entrance ready to be immediately raised when needed.

The chain had to be supported on lighters when in position and it was kept taught by capstans on both sides of the harbour. The capstan on the Portsmouth side was located adjacent to the Round Tower on the west side in Capstan Square and was still there in 1843. [10]

Capstan Square © of the British Library Board.

In 1930 workmen raised several links of the "mightie chaine of yren" whilst excavating to the east of the Round Tower. One of these links was placed in Portsmouth Museum and the links measured 3ft 9ins in length and were 3ins thick, and are thought to be from the 1664 chaine. [14]

In the early twentieth century a boom defence comprising a number of timber struts secured by steel hawsers, each approximately 30ft long with steel spikes, was deployed across the harbour entrance, with a central section that could be towed away. Unfortunately a Dockyard launch was swept on to the structure by the tide and was holed.

A similar boom was deployed in the First World War with an anti-submarine net that could be raised. There was an engine and fairleads located in the site of what is today the Boomyard of the Portsmouth Sailing Club, to tension this harbour defence.

Deploying the boom in Portsmouth Harbour entrance by W. L. Wyllie
© National Maritime Museum Greenwich.

In 1926 Portsmouth was granted city status following a long campaign by the Borough Council. The application was made on the grounds that Portsmouth was the "first naval port of the kingdom. In 1929 the city council added the motto "Heaven's Light Our Guide" to the medieval coat of arms. Further changes were made to the arms in 1970, when the Portsmouth Museums Trust sponsored the grant of crest, supporters and heraldic badge. The crest and supporters are based on those of the royal arms, but altered to show the city's maritime connections: the lions and unicorn have been given fish tails, and a naval crown placed around the latter animal. Around the unicorn is wrapped a representation of "The Mighty Chain of Iron", a Tudor defensive boom across Portsmouth Harbour.

The history of the Mighty chain appears to demonstrate the difficulty of deploying and maintaining such heavy harbour defences at a time when appropriate technology was unavailable, and its suitability and effectiveness is questionable, although its intended purpose is very plausible.

The Square Tower

The Square Tower, together with the Round Tower and Saluting Platform, were among the first defences to be constructed and these three structures are the only parts of the Tudor works that survive today. The Square Tower was built in 1494, and although it was part of the fortifications, it was also designed for domestic life, since it is thought to have housed the military governor at some time.

On the north side of the Square Tower is a replica of a bust of King Charles Ist presented to the town and recessed into the Tower wall facing up High Street. The inscription reads:

After his travels through all France and Spain, and having passed very many dangers by sea and land, he arrived here on the 5th day of October 1623 and originally ended "there was the greatest applause of joy for his safety throughout the kingdom that was ever known or heard of."

The inscription appears to have been mutilated in the early years of the nineteenth century.

The bust of King Charles I inset in the wall of the Square Tower.

At the end of the sixteenth or early seventeenth century the building was adapted as a magazine but by 1716 it was thought to be unsuitable for this purpose due to the fact gunpowder was left on the streets when transporting it to the hoys (boats) on Point.

It was reported that:

> Broad Street in war time is the popular part of town, and at shipping of the powder from Point among a crowd of drunken smoking sailors tending the Men of War's boats is also a very great hazard. When funerals pass the Magazine it was claimed that the sparks of the links and torches have been seen to fly against the walls and windows of the building, and as this building is sited next to the sea and within reach of shipping makes it a very good mark to bombard where 6000 barrels of powder are lodged. [10]

However the building continued in use as a magazine for many more years and a wooden jetty known as the Powder Bridge was constructed on the site of the current Victoria Pier, in order to reduce the risk to the population of transporting gunpowder through the streets. Access to the jetty was via a sally port.

Around 1777, the gunpowder store in the Square Tower was transferred to Priddy's Hard, Gosport, to a purpose made building, the first time that gunpowder stores had been separated from ordnance stores in Britain. At the same time, other ordnance stores were concentrated in Weevil Lane, Gosport, to the south of Priddy's Hard. [77]

The Square Tower in 1729. *"History of Portsmouth, a Naval Chronology"* by William. G. Gates. Reproduced courtesy of *The News Portsmouth.*

As the fleet grew, victualling became very important, and numerous premises were acquired and used for this reason in Old Portsmouth. Therefore, in 1779 it was proposed that the Square Tower would be more appropriately used for this purpose, so the old magazine became a meat store, used in conjunction with the newly-erected slaughter house nearby, to transport fresh meat to the navy's ships. Following this change the Powder Bridge was renamed "The Beef Stage".

In 1823 the Admiralty established a semaphore station on top of the Square Tower to communicate with the ships at sea and it also became the first of a chain of towers linking Portsmouth with the Admiralty in London.

The stations between Portsmouth and London were Portsdown, Beacon Hill, Blackdown, Hascombe, Netley Heath, Cabbage Hill, Putney and Chelsea. It was claimed a message could be sent in 30 minutes on a clear day.

This semaphore tower was itself made redundant by the introduction of the electric telegraph and was demolished in 1848.

The Semaphore in 1830 and the guns of the Saluting Battery and houses in Battery Row. © National Maritime Museum Greenwich.

Between 1848-50 the whole of the defences were reorganised. The Square Tower was returned to the Board of Ordnance and the top of the building reinforced with concrete to support three eight inch guns.

Other fortifications

In 1547 Edward Vaughan who came to Portsmouth as its appointed Captain, complained of the weakness of the town, particularly mentioning the weakness of Point Gate, (presumably this was the original gate and was not very substantial):

> I do not dout that your lordships doth ryght well consydre the estate of thys towne and how it lyeth open, so that at lowe water men cum into yt although they were 30 in rank, and also, the gate to the water side (Point Gate) are so weake, that 4 or 5 good fellows with a piece of tymber may lay them on the ground, and the walls, with thys frost that hathe been of late, doth mowther away and begynnyth in divers places to fall into the dyke. [9]

Two maps showing Portsmouth's defences were produced in 1542 and 1568 and they show that Point changed little between the two dates, with the exception of a wall that ran from the Round Tower to the Square Tower and beyond. This is well illustrated in the Cowdray Print of 1545, on which part of the wall can be seen as a wooden and gabion defence work erected after 1542, probably during the invasion crisis of 1545.

The map of 1542 shows a timber fence – thought to have been erected in the fifteenth century, between Point Gate and the Round Tower, which is referred to as "The Pales" on a later map.

In August 1560 Richard Popynjay was appointed Surveyor of Portsmouth and started to redesign many aspects of its fortifications, although much delay was caused by the Plague, which came to Portsmouth in 1563, causing many deaths. [9]

To pay for the necessary works Queen Elizabeth I inaugurated the first state lottery with tickets going on sale from 1566 and the draw took place in 1569.

400,000 tickets were sold at 10 shillings each, with the first prize being valued £5000, comprising £3000 cash, £700 worth of plate and the remainder in tapestries and linens. There were twenty five prizes of £100 and all subscribers got back half a crown. [9]

In fact, it is thought that a substantial Point Gate (sometimes called Poynt Gate) was built sometime after 1586, consisting of a flat wall across the neck of Point peninsular, with a large gateway in its centre and two square bulwarks at each end of the wall.

It appears that the "new" gateway of 1687 was not in fact an original construction but that a new façade was given to an existing gateway.

It was the first of Portsmouth's great ornamental gates, being called King James's Gate and dated 1687, the year of King James II's visit to Portsmouth. [9]

This gate was in the Venetian style with double Corinthian pilasters on each side the archway with an entablature supporting a circular tower and ball and ornamental spires on each side.

King James's Gate as originally built. *"History of Portsmouth, a Naval Chronology"* by William Gates. Reproduced courtesy of The News Portsmouth.

Later modification with additional entrance included c.1884 just before its demolition. *"Illustrated History of Portsmouth"* by W. G. Gates. Reproduced courtesy of The News Portsmouth.

Charles II appointed the Dutch Sir Bernard De Gomme his Chief Engineer of all the King's castles in England and Wales, and in 1665 sent him to Portsmouth to commence a major rebuilding programme of the town's defences, which involved remodelling the ramparts and bastions, widening existing moats, and building others.

Much of De Gomme's work, implemented over a period of more than twenty years, was carried out by Dutch prisoners.

In addition to improvements to the existing defences, he built the Eighteen gun battery between the Round Tower and the Square Tower in the 1680s and a further battery to the east of the Square Tower. Henry VIII had in fact previously built some temporary defences, fashioned out of timber with gabions along the outer edge, at the site of the Eighteen gun battery in around 1540.

However, at the end of the Eighteen gun battery he cut through the neck of the peninsular with a moat to the north of the gateway (later King James's Gate) between the sea and the Camber.

This act really put the rapidly expanding Portsmouth Point, or Spice Island, "without "or geographically outside the city walls, a factor which was to contribute to its notorious reputation in the eighteenth and nineteenth centuries.

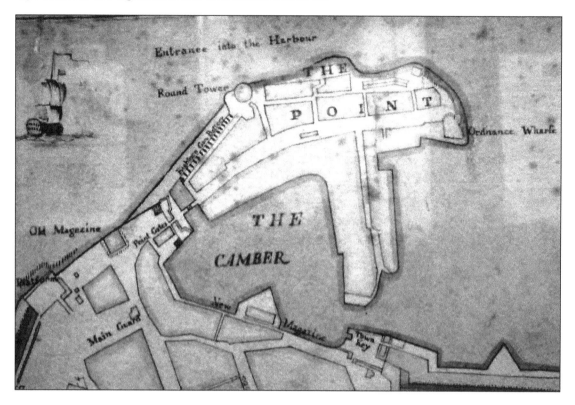

This old map (late seventeenth century) clearly shows the bridge between Point and the town of Portsmouth.

There was a massive drawbridge built in front of the gate on the line of Broad Street, but sometime during the eighteenth century a caponier was built across the south end of the moat to provide a means of communication between the Point defences and the town during an assault.

This, however, would have been built for military purposes only and the gate and drawbridge would have continued to control civilian traffic. In practice the drawbridge would have been used less and less as time passed, especially as utilities such as water and gas would have had to pass over it and was eventually replaced by a permanent bridge.

William Gates suggests that the gate was demolished shortly after 1860 and its façade reconstructed on the Burnaby Road frontage of the old United Officers Recreation Ground.

De Gomme had also erected a small bastion in 1687, known as the Camber bastion, which stuck out from the old Tudor wall in the Inner Camber, with circular portholes commanding the drawbridge. Originally a magazine was built on the bastion and later in 1833-34 it was replaced by a new military hospital.

The two drawings above produced c.1716 by John Turner show the New Magazine built on the Camber Bastion and are copied from the original drawings of C. Lampreriere. The upper drawing is viewed from the Town Key and in the background can be see the Isle of Wight and the Old Magazine (Square Tower) with the Point Gate and drawbridge on the right. The lower drawing viewed from the Point Gate clearly shows the Town Key and Town wall. © The British Library Board.

Sally Ports

The construction of Eighteen gun battery necessitated the provision of a means of accessing Point beach (known today as Sally Port beach) from the landward. De Gomme therefore constructed a sally port, a narrow passageway with an S bend to ensure the battery could not be rushed by an assault party from the beach.

This sally port was outside the town and sited to the north of King James's Gate. It became the principal naval landing place of the port at one time and officers and boat's crew would frequently land and embark there to save the long pull, or sail, in or out of the harbour.

Innumerable heroes embarked there to fight their country's battles and have returned with the spoils of victory.

This sally port was the embarkation point for the "First Fleet" that left Portsmouth to sail to Australia in 1787.

However, as Naval activity increased in the eighteenth century, Point beach became extensively used for trafficking with the fleet anchored at Spithead and this single sally port became very inconvenient. Therefore, towards the end of the century, a casemate in the centre of the battery was opened up to give improved access to the beach, and at about the same time, a completely new water gate and landing stage was constructed east of St James's Gate, between the gate and the Square Tower, and became known as the "New Sally Port "or" King's Stairs."

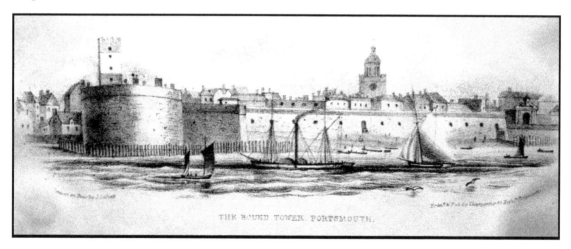

THE ROUND TOWER, PORTSMOUTH.

This lithograph is one of a series published by Charpentier of Portsmouth High Street c. 1830s, showing different harbour entrance views. The casemate which was opened up in the centre of Eighteen Gun Battery as a sally port and still used today, is clearly visible, as is the original sally port to the north of King James's gate at the eastern end of the battery.

This new entrance allowed access into the fortress town, unlike the other sally ports and it appears to have been reserved for important visitors and naval officers and later was used by passengers waiting to board the Portsmouth to Ryde steam packet from Victoria Pier.

In 1847 the properties that existed between Eighteen gun battery and Broad Street , which included a number of notorious pubs, were demolished to allow "Point Barracks" to be constructed.

The construction of Point Barracks allowed modifications to be carried out to Eighteen gun battery and provide a barracks for artillerymen.

Most of the modifications were carried out in brick and the main block of the artillery barracks was sited at the western end of the battery between Broad Street and the Round Tower.

However, these improvements to the fortifications and the construction of Point Barracks resulted in the casemate in the centre of Eighteen gun battery (now a sally port) being restored to its original function and De Gomme's sally port at the eastern end of the battery was also sealed off. In addition the Camber moat was filled in and the break in the seawall between the end of Eighteen gun battery and the King James's Gate defences was made good with matching stone. [10]

The loss of these two sally ports caused great upset to the watermen and townspeople, who regarded this a loss of public rights and a recognised launching place for watermen and others. After much protestation they were eventually allowed to use the naval sally port.

The old town defences which had developed over a period of 500 years became redundant, and many were systematically demolished in the late nineteenth century. However the seaward line of the city's defences remained, where guns could be deployed to protect the approaches to and from the harbour entrance during the Second World War.

Finally, the Portsmouth Garrison was dissolved in 1960 and the City Council acquired the remainder of the city's defences from the M.O.D, which it maintains to the present day.

Point Barracks were screened from Broad Street by a high brick wall which was ultimately demolished in 1962-63, opening up the area to the public. Shortly afterwards the sally port in the centre of Eighteen gun battery was reopened and is still in use today.

The fortifications and beach c.1950 clearly showing the sally port opening in Eighteen Gun Battery and one of the existing sally ports near the Square Tower.

The fortifications on Point are still extremely impressive and are a very popular tourist attraction but today their main function is primarily as part of the city's sea defences, protecting the Point area from flooding and coastal erosion, much as they used to protect it from invasion and foreign attack.

Chapter 3

Crime, Cruelty and Punishment on Point

Prostitution

Between the seventeenth and nineteenth centuries, Portsmouth Point attained notoriety throughout the seafaring world for its uniqueness as a place where anything could be traded and pubs and prostitutes were plentiful to satisfy seamen's needs ashore after paying off from a long voyage. The Portsmouth prostitutes were known during that time as "Point Beachers" to seamen.

Many of these prostitutes would not think twice about swindling a sailor and robbing him and an article published in the *Country News* in June 1757 tells of an incident that befell an unfortunate woman on the Point.
This particular woman was mistakenly identified by a sailor as a prostitute from Point who had robbed him the day before of ten Johannes (Portuguese gold coin). Together with some of his shipmates they took from her three gold rings and stripped her naked and ducked her in the sea several times before forcing her to walk home in the middle of the day through the streets. It turned out that she was innocent of the crime and efforts were subsequently made to find and apprehend the barbarians.

One can appreciate the reason for this unfortunate incident when another article in a newspaper in the early nineteenth century reports that:

> This morning three ladies of pleasure who hung out at the back of the Point were sent to Winchester gaol for wheedling a poor countryman into their infernal residence, intoxicating him and robbing him of 14 guineas and 14 shillings.

In 1795 Dr George Pinckard was appointed an Army doctor, and in that capacity he sailed in the "*Ulysses*" from Portsmouth on 15th November, returning to Portsmouth after two weeks of storms, before finally setting off for the West Indies on 31st December 1795.

Whilst visiting Portsmouth at this time he made the following comments about the local prostitutes:

> In respect to streets, houses, markets and traffic, Portsmouth is not unlike other towns, but Portsmouth Point, Portsea Common and some other parts of the town have peculiarities which seem to sanction the celebrity the place has acquired.
> In some quarters Portsmouth is not only filthy, and crowded with a class of low and abandoned beings, who seem to have declared open war against every habit of common decency and decorum... The riotous, drunken and immoral scenes of this place, perhaps, exceed all others.

Commonly gross obscenity and intoxication preserve enough of diffidence to seek the concealment of the night, but here hordes of profligate females are seen reeling in drunkenness, or plying upon the streets in open say with a broad immodesty which puts the great orb of noon to the blush.

To form to yourself an idea of these tender, languishing nymphs, these lovely fighting ornaments of the fair sex, imagine something of more than Amazonian stature, having a crimson countenance, emblazoned with all the effrontery of Cyprian confidence and broad Bacchanalian folly; give to her bold countenance the warlike features of two wounded cheeks, a tumid nose, scarred and battered brows, and a pair of blackened eyes, with balls of red; then add to her sides a pair of brawny arms, fit to encounter a Colossus and her upon two ankles like the fixed supporters of a gate.

Afterwards, by way of apparel, put upon her a loose flying cap, a man's black hat, a torn neckerchief, stone rings on her fingers, and a dirty white, or tawdry flowered gown with short apron, and a pink petticoat; and thus you will have something very like the figure of a "Portsmouth Poll."

Callous to every sense of shame, these daring objects reel about the streets, lie in wait at the corners, or, like the devouring kite, hover over every landing place, eager to pounce upon their prey, and each unhappy tar, who has the misfortune to fall under their talons, has no hope of escape till plucked of every feather.

The instant he sets foot on dry land he is embraced by the neck, hugged around the waist, or hooked in the arms by one or more of those tender Dulcineas, and thus poor Jack, with pockets full of prize money, or rich with the wages of a long and dangerous cruise, is instantly dragged (though it must be confessed not always against his consent) to a bagnio , or some filthy pot house where he is kept drinking, smoking, singing, dancing, swearing and rioting, amidst one continual scene of debauchery, all day and all night and all night and all day until his every farthing has gone.

He is then left to sleep till he is sober, and awakes to return, penniless, to his ship, with much cause to think himself fortunate if an empty purse be the worst consequence of his long wished for ramble ashore.

The following old adage frequently quoted: - "Sailors earn money like horses and spend it like asses" would seem to have been very appropriate in this context.

A coloured etching by Thomas Rowlandson dated 1809 entitled *"Launching a Frigate"*. The picture depicts a young woman beginning her career as a prostitute and compares it to the launching of a frigate. It shows an interesting contrast between the Madam and the prostitute. © Victoria and Albert Museum, London.

William Robinson was a seaman in the Royal Navy who wrote a book entitled: *"Jack Nastyface, memoirs of a seaman"* which described his time aboard ship between 1805 and 1811. The following extract from his book describes events aboard having just dropped anchor in Spithead:

> After having moored our ship, swarms of boats came around us; some were what are generally termed bomb-boats (bumboats), but are really nothing but floating chandler's shops, and a great many of them were freighted with cargoes of ladies. A sight that was truly gratifying, and a great treat; for our crew consisting of six hundred and upwards, nearly all young men, had seen but one woman on board for 18 months.
> So soon as these boats were allowed to come alongside, the seamen flocked down pretty quick, one after the other, and brought their choice up, so that in the course of the afternoon we had about 450 on board.
> Of all the human race, these poor young creatures are the most pitiable; the ill usage and the degradation they are driven to submit to are indescribable; but from habit they become callous, indifferent as to the delicacy of speech and behaviour, and so totally lost to all sense of shame, that they seem to retain no quality which properly belongs to women, but the shape and name. Thus these unfortunates are taken to market like cattle; and, whilst this system is observed, it cannot with truth be said, that the slave-trade is abolished in England.

"Cattle not Insurable" 1809 by Thomas Rowlandson
© National Gallery of Art, Washington D C.

This drawing beautifully depicts prostitutes being ferried to and from Men of War anchored at Spithead. The title appropriately suggests what the scene must have been like in these times when hordes of women were brought alongside in wherries to clamber aboard to ply their trade with jolly jack tar.

In 1813 a humorous Poem was written entitled *"JACK JUNK* or *The Sailors Cruize on Shore"* by William Henry Ireland.

The Book was dedicated to every Jack Tar in The British Navy and describes in verse the time Jack has ashore when returning to Portsmouth from a 5 year voyage in the East Indies.

From his vessel anchored in Spithead he comes ashore at Capstan Square, Point, with more than £100 to spend where he and his crew mates are met by numerous prostitutes, and they then enter the first pub *"The Jolly Sailor"* where drinking and dancing commences.
The poems describe Jack's escapades over several days as he travels in Portsmouth, and beyond to Portchester, visiting numerous drinking houses with women in tow, and meeting up with his mess mates and lasses before they eventually arrive back at Point.

The description of the prostitute's names in the book are very amusing:

Now bearing up at Capstan Square,

Choice dainty lasses greet em there,

Bet Stride her ruby color show;

Sal Walker sports her bowsprit nose;

Nan Brag her bulky breeching rears;

Pol Sherwin shows the bottles tears;

And last, for fam'd for fisty prize;

Mol Chantress view with bung'd up eyes.

Now beating up at Capstan Square
Choice dainty Damsels greet 'em there.

Drawing of Jack's arrival at Capstan Square.

After fighting breaks out in one pub called "*The Naked Boy*", the constables arrest Jack and his mates, who then escape but are later re arrested and end up in the local guardhouse penniless and injured.

Jack and his mess mates are taken back aboard his ship at Spithead and they are reunited with the prostitutes who were rowed to the ship by a local wherryman.

After three weeks on board the women are rowed ashore and Jack prepares to set sail again, knowing that in his brief time ashore he had spent all of his £100.
Again this demonstrates what was probably not an unusual shore excursion for sailors after paying off from their ships, frittering away their hard earned wages in a short space of time.

Admiral Edward Hawker was another who made observations of the appalling behaviour of prostitutes brought aboard ship and he published an anonymous pamphlet in 1821.

He referred to the Portsmouth prostitutes as being hard bitten, drunken and debauched and called them "Spithead Nymphs."

The conditions below deck were overcrowded aboard without these extra women but when they arrived it was filled to overflowing.

Bearing in mind that the space allowed each man for his hammock was 16 inches breadth so that when women were aboard, the dirt, filth and stench were appalling and all were witness to each other's actions being so close to each other. It was the case sometimes that men took two women aboard making it even more crowded.

With more men than women aboard, men and women are in sight of each other shamelessly and unblushingly coupling like dogs.

These descriptions and stories about the Point prostitutes at that time go some way to show what levels people will sink to survive or pleasure themselves and what a den of iniquity Point was during that era.

Bullbaiting and other cruel sports.

In the mid seventeenth century there was a small row of houses, of about 150 feet long which was situated in the centre of Broad Street, nearly opposite the *Blue Posts*, and was known as Fisherman's Row or Middle Houses. [5] It is likely that these properties were some of the first constructed on this shingle spit and were built by fishermen on the highest land on the spit to provide some protection from the tidal flooding that has always occurred here. It is also likely that their boats would have been moored in the Camber nearby.

The four properties were bought in April 1771 by the Portsmouth Corporation for the sum of £300, of which £130 was raised by voluntary subscriptions, to allow Broad Street to be widened. [11] At one end of Fisherman's Row was situated an iron ring placed in the ground at which it was customary on every Shrove Tuesday to bait a bull.

Bull baiting was popular throughout the Middle Ages and well into the eighteenth century and was patronised by all classes of people, from the rich to the poor, including priests. Indeed almost every town and village in England had a bull ring at some point.

Shrove Tuesday was traditionally a day on which people confessed in order to be better prepared for the observation of the ensuing season of penitence and for receiving the sacrament at Easter.

It was later converted to a day of idle sports and amusements and it was soon distinguished by riot and drunkenness, bull baiting, cock fighting and other cruel pastimes.

Bullbaiting involved tethering the bull with a collar and rope long enough to allow it some mobility, and then setting ferocious dogs on it until it was weakened and bloodied from fighting. The bull was then slaughtered by butchers.

Bull baiting.

Cock throwing was another game traditionally played on Shrove Tuesday and on other festive occasions and the game began with the tethering of a cock to a stake with about a foot or two of slack in the rope. The contestants then took turns at throwing clubs at the cock until it was dead.

Cock fighting was another cruel pastime practiced across the country in the eighteenth century and a cock pit was known to have existed in the *Blue Anchor* public house situated at the southern end of Broad Street

Typical scene showing a cock fight arena with a fight in progress.

In February 1720 the following Public Notice was published in Portsmouth against the throwing of cocks:

> Whereas riots, quarrels, and other mischiefs are often occasioned and do arise at and by the barbarous usuage of throwing at cocks, the Mayor and his Justices do therefore prohibit all persons whosoever from assembling together within the said Burrough or the Libertys thereof for that purpose, and do hereby give notice that whatsoever person or persons shall be there found any way acting or assisting in throwing at cocks shall be punished for such offence as severely as by law they may. [11]

By the end of the eighteenth century many towns were enforcing ordinances against cock fighting and bullbaiting. Municipal Ordinances were followed in 1835 by the Cruelty to Animals Act, which outlawed the "running", baiting or fighting of any animal which included cock fighting and dog fighting.

After the Shrove Tuesday bullbaiting was abolished, the more humane pastime of trying to catch a greasy pig was introduced in Bath Square during regatta festivities. F.J. Proctor in his book "*Reminiscences of Old Portsmouth*" described the event as follows:

> Only boys were allowed to compete, and the only way they could secure the prize was by grasping a foreleg with one hand, and finger looping the curly tail with the other hand. This was a very difficult exercise and often the boys were covered in grease as the excited pig tried to escape through the crowds with women screaming in fear of soiling their long dresses. After many attempts, a fortunate competitor would catch the pig and carry off the wriggling screaming animal.

Another barbarous activity that "Pointers" used to participate in at the early part of the seventeenth century was that of anointing rats with turpentine and setting them alight. At the Quarter Sessions in 1704 a presentation was made by the Grand Jury against this cruel practice, not, be it observed, because it was abominable cruelty of the act, but through fear that the lighted rodents might fire one of the magazines that existed at that time on Point. [5]

Punishments

History has shown us that some punishments centuries ago were really barbaric and Point was no different in this respect and the cage, prison, whipping post, pillory and stocks were all in use in Portsmouth.

Stocks

Pillorie

Whipping post

In 1569 at the Sessions, a "payne" (instruction to carry out a duty), was given to the Chamberlains to repair the prison, the cage and the stocks for the punishment of criminal offenders in the town.

Fines were given out to Chamberlains for not carrying out these instructions. One Chamberlain named Thomas Lardnor neglected to provide a pillory and was fined 30 shillings in 1620, and on another occasion in 1622.

Lardnor was fined again by the court in for not making up a "pair of stocks", "sufficient cage", "cuckinge stool" and "pillorie."

Cuckinge stool

A cuckinge (cucking) or ducking stool was a chair used for punishment of disorderly women in an act of public humiliation. Stocks partially immobilised offenders, and they were often exposed in a public place to humiliate the offender.

A pillory was a wooden framework on a post with holes for the head and hands into which offenders were firmly locked in order to be exposed to public scorn.

The pillory was not in common use and the seriousness of the crime dictated the punishment. Some prisoners were not molested by the populace, but others were pelted with missiles. For example in April 1803 a man who had outraged a child was bombarded in the pillory by spectators hurling mud, rotten eggs and oranges etc. The last recorded use of a pillory was in March 1814.

Records show that in 1687 the Chamberlain was instructed to make the cage and pillory strong and sufficient to contain a body of any person. Stocks were also erected on Point at this time, and the other instruments were probably close by.

Stocks were maintained and still used in the nineteenth century in certain parts of Portsmouth.

In *East's Records of Portsmouth* it is stated that during the years 1698-1781 no less than 120 men and 98 women were publicly whipped. Some of these offenders were vagrants found begging and the remainder were mainly for felony or petty larceny. The accused male or female were whipped with a "catt of nine Tayls" after being stripped from the waist upwards, receiving the punishment on the naked back until his or her body was bloody.

Whipping posts were installed at a number of locations in the town where the sentence was carried out or the prisoner was tied to the back of a cart and flogged from one part of the Borough to another, such as from the Gaol to the end of Point and back.

Records still exist of some of the Constables' bills in which charges for whipping appear [11]:

For example Constable Edmonds' bill from October 1698 includes the following:

January 7th for whipping a man   6d

January 9th for whipping a man and woman   1s

From his bill in 1699 he claims

January 3rd for whipping 2 women and lame man and taking all to Gosport.   2s

Public whippings continued for many years until the last public whippings in Portsmouth on January 11th 1816.

The original gaol was known as the Whitehouse and was not far from Point, being situated in the High Street.

The conditions in this gaol, which at one time temporarily held "Jack the Painter," were extremely poor and in October 1714 three women prisoners petitioned the Mayor, pleading that "lying on the bordes tis hard and cold and full of rats." They sought his pity and requested their liberty to get bread as they were weak with cold and hunger.

"Jack the Painter" was responsible for the burning of Plymouth and Portsmouth Dockyards in 1766 and was found guilty and later executed by hanging from a gibbet outside the Dockyard gates and his body was later suspended on chains on Blockhouse Point at the entrance to the harbour. Early in the nineteenth century a new gaol was built in Penny Street. [5]

Last flogging of a British soldier at Point/Artillery Barracks, Broad St.

This was the place where the last official flogging of a British soldier took place.
The following description is an account of that distressing scene: "The nature of the culprit's offence was unknown to me, but he was strapped to a gun carriage, and his back received the cat o' nine tales till his back was bloody."

The local Press took the matter up with their accustomed desire for legitimised reform and the War Office was bombarded with protests, which paved the way to the repeal of this form of punishment, especially because it was inflicted at times for what today would be considered minor or even trivial lapses of military discipline. [4]

Chapter 4

Pubs, Taverns and Hotels

The first pubs on Spice Island were built in the early seventeenth century, not long after the first buildings were constructed and records indicate that by 1610, four inns had appeared along Broad Street and the road layout was also starting to take shape. [1]

A detailed map made by Bernarde de Gomme in 1668 indicates the main road being called High Street (Broad Street today) and the streets that became East Street, Bath Square and Tower Street can be clearly seen, although they are not named.

Once King James's gate was constructed in 1687, replacing the Poynt gate, Point was "outside" the fortified town of Portsmouth and this contributed to its notorious reputation in the eighteenth and nineteenth centuries.

One of the earliest known pubs was the *White Lyon* or *White Lion*, detailed as being sited near Poynt Gate in 1607.

The road network on Spice Island expanded in the early years and with the building of Bathing House Square, East Street and Tower Street came more pubs: by 1716, 41 pubs were recorded on Spice Island, in addition to numerous beer houses. [11]

With the ever growing naval presence and other sailors and merchants arriving from around the world, it is therefore no wonder that Spice Island achieved its world famous notoriety. The pubs were the centre of Spice Island's iniquity, becoming famed for their scenes of rioting and debauchery and the associated entertainments of prostitution, gambling and cruel sports.

At one time Portsmouth was said to have more pubs to the square yard than any other place in the country, with the number of pubs on Spice Island reaching its peak during the eighteenth and nineteenth centuries. [15]

The following Portsmouth Annual Directories list the numbers of public houses in existence at that time on the Point:-

Sadler's Hampshire Directory	1784	47
Pigot & Co.'s. National Commercial Directory.	1823-24.	45
" " " " "	1830.	47
Pigot & Co's. Directory of Portsmouth.	1844.	41
Slater's Directory of Portsmouth.	1851.	29

"Dispatch or Jack preparing for sea" by Thomas Rowlandson 1810 © National Maritime Museum, Greenwich, London, shows Jack enjoying himself ashore with a couple of prostitutes.

DISPATCH OR JACK PREPARING FOR SEA

Since Portsmouth was the home of the Royal Navy, ships of the fleet were continuously coming and going, being anchored in Spithead before and after voyages, with crews coming ashore at the Sally Port, Capstan Square and at Point to spend their wages, or perhaps prize money from foreign ships captured.

Sometimes this prize money was very significant, although not very fairly shared between the crew and officers, and the lure of the pubs, prostitutes and gambling were available to help them spend it.

> Scarcely any locality was known to contain so many houses of entertainment as Point, and most of these houses were named after great victories and celebrated fighting ships. The main street had its *Royal George, Arethusa, Ship Worcester*, and *Neptune & Mars*. Bathing House Square had its *Quebec* and *Roving Sailor*, and Capstan Square had its notorious *Lord Hood* and *Ship Tyger*, whilst the famous *Blue Posts* in Broad Street should not be forgotten. [16]

Among the most famous pubs on Point were the following: - the *Quebec Hotel*, *Still and West*, *Blue Posts Hotel*, *Star and Garter*, *Blue Anchor* and *Prince William Henry*.

Quebec Hotel

The *Quebec Hotel* was sited in Bathing House Square (now known as Bath Square.) It was named Bathing House Square after the bathing house that was built there in 1754, the construction of which was advertised in a local newspaper on Jan 28th of that year:-

> Yesterday the workmen drove the first pile for erecting a salt water Bathing House, on Portsmouth Point, in the presence of the Right Worshipful Mayor, several of the Aldermen,

Burgesses, Gentlemen, and a great number of other persons, who all testified their approbation by giving three huzzas. A handsome present was made to the workmen, to drink success to the undertaking, and when completed, it will be the most commodious and convenient Saltwater Bathing House in this Kingdom. [17]

The site immediately north of, and adjacent to the bathing house, was first leased in April 1755, and it is likely that the current *Quebec House*, originally a single storey bathing house, was later absorbed, or possibly built or rebuilt as part of the *Quebec tavern* in the 1780s when the tavern was erected, or shortly afterwards.

The name Quebec presumably commemorates Wolfe's victory in 1759, since the forces sailed from Portsmouth and afterwards the body of General Wolfe was brought ashore at Point with full naval and military honours:

> ## PASSAGE TO HAVRE-DE-GRACE.
>
> THE moment the French Ports are open the following Vessels will sail from PORTSMOUTH to HAVRE-DE-GRACE, and continue so to do every week, and carry Passengers and Goods upon the most reasonable terms, viz.
>
> Schooner CHARLOTTE, burthen Ninety Tons, with twelve Beds in the great Cabin.
>
> Sloop ANT, burthen Forty Tons.
>
> Both which Vessels are capital Sailers, and are handsomely and conveniently fitted up for the accommodation of Ladies and Gentlemen going to France. Distance only about ten hours sail.
>
> Enquire at Mr. CROSS's, Crown Inn, High-street; or Capt. STEPHENS, Quebec Tavern, near the Bathing-House, on the Point.

The hotel was extremely popular and was well used by people alighting on boats for travel to foreign countries. One of the tavern's adverts appeared in the *Hampshire Telegraph* in December 1803 thus:

> ### FOR SALE BY AUCTION,
>
> On THURSDAY, the 20th of January, 1803, between the hours of 5 and 7 o'clock in the evening, at the sign of the West India and Quebec Tavern, on Portsmouth Point,
>
>  THE following VESSELS: the Schooner CHARLOTTE, 76 tons per register,
>
> | | Feet | Inches |
> |---|---|---|
> | Length | 59 | 10 |
> | Breadth | 17 | 5 |
> | Depth in Hold | 8 | 0 |
>
> About two years and a half old, in excellent repair, and well found in every necessary Article, fitted up in a very handsome manner for a Packet, having 12 bed cabins, with their beds and furniture compleat, and ready for Sea at a moment's notice.
>
> Also the Smack LARK, about 28 tons per register, in good order, and well found, fit for any trade of a Vessel of her size.
>
> Also the Sloop MARY ANN, 21 tons per register, in good order, and calculated for conveying horses or other cattle.
>
> For further particulars apply to Mr. RICHARD STEPHENS, at the above Tavern.

The hotel was also a popular place for auctions of boats and associated marine equipment.

It was very popular with travellers embarking for India during the early part of the nineteenth century by which time the name had been changed to the *West India and Quebec Tavern*.

Quebec Hotel, with bathing house in the foreground seen as a single storey building c.1828.

In 1837 the hotel took in a number of rescued passengers from the vessel *Colonist* after she had caught fire at Spithead on her way to India. Many of the passengers were women and children who had lost all their possessions. [15]
In 1838 the tavern and bathing house were linked and the former bathing house was being used at this time as a storehouse and counting house.

By 1840 it was the point of departure for Ryde's steam packets to the Isle of Wight and the hotel was a staging point for coaches to and from London, with timings of coaches such that passengers could then take connections to continue their journey by water. Some adverts also mentioned that warm and cold baths were available in the house.

The *Quebec Hotel* was well known as being one of the most famous inns in Old Portsmouth for sailors, fishermen, stage coach drivers and smugglers." [5] In connection with smuggling there was a tale of a secret waterway, or passage, beneath the building, reputedly communicating with the *Still and West* and the *Old Blue Posts,* although I am unaware of any evidence of this.

In 1845 the last fatal duel was fought in England, and one of the two protagonists, Capt. Seton of the 11th Dragoons, was brought here injured and subsequently died. Following the court case and the great sensation it created, duelling was banned and became illegal. [5]

The *Quebec Hotel* is last listed as a hotel in 1859, and by 1862 it was under the ownership of Messrs Pickford & Co, Carriers, and remained so, well into the twentieth century.
The main hotel building was demolished c.1920.

Still and West

Another pub, which has become world famous, is the *Still and West* situated in Bath Square at the harbour entrance, originally known at the *Still Tavern* and constructed around 1733.

The current pub name was adopted when the daughter of the owner of the *East and West Country House* located nearby, married the owner of the *Still Tavern* in 1882.

At the end of the nineteenth century and early twentieth century, regular fish markets were held outside with the pub opening at 4am and closing at 11pm. The catch was brought ashore here with baskets dragged over the sea wall nearby, part of which still exists today and there used to be timber steps leading down to the beach.

> The fishmongers of Point auctioned the catches in lots to suit the hawkers, who did a roaring trade. But when the facilities of rail transport increased, and the fishing grounds shifted to other parts of the coast, the fish market flourished no longer, and the busy sights I have seen gradually vanished, save as a memory of sturdy men shouting out prices amid the bustle, itinerant salesmen elbowing to the front for an early chance of securing choice lots, and carts and barrows clattering over the cobbled stones. [4]

The *Still and West* in the early twentieth century when the fish markets were still being held.

One of the local fish merchants in Bath Square, W. H. Hooper & Sons.

Some of the fishmongers used to meet the fish train that arrived from Billingsgate at 5am and collect the fish in their horse and carts before bringing them to the Point market at 6am to sell.

Although not one of the primary coaching inns on the Point, in the early nineteenth century coaches travelling to London used to call at the *Still and West* every evening to collect passengers.

The *Still and West* was in the national news in August 1960 when the last British Battleship *HMS Vanguard* was being towed out of Portsmouth harbour to the breakers yard and went aground not far from the pub. Fortunately the ship was stopped from doing any damage, and was pulled off by her tugs allowing her to continue on her journey.

This pub is still thriving today and is particularly popular during the summer months when visitors and tourists enjoy its hospitality and spectacular views of the harbour.

Blue Posts Hotel

One of the most famous hotels and oldest houses in Broad Street was the *Blue Posts Hotel*, originally built in 1613 and frequented by young naval officers.

It was the principal coaching inn on the Point and indeed all the coaches, vans and waggons to London and other places started from it and in the early years of the nineteenth century at least 20 coaches came out of Portsmouth daily, as well as the Royal Mail every night.

It was known for the very large porch at its entrance which was supported by two massive columns painted blue. This hotel was where the author Marryat had his *Peter Simple* duel.

Peter Simple was a novel written by Captain Marryat in the nineteenth century about a young 15 year old very inexperienced and naïve midshipman who on his arrival in Portsmouth stayed at the Blue Posts hotel for a while. Whilst there he managed to have a disagreement with a fellow midshipman resulting in a duel that was fought at the rear of the premises. On the morning of the duel he was very concerned that he may be shot, but was tricked by his fellow midshipmen who loaded the guns with powder, and no shot, without him knowing, and he only discovered this sometime after the event, since when firing he closed his eyes and shot in the air.

In addition to being the most well-known coaching inn on the Point, the *Blue Posts* was regularly used as a meeting place and an auction house, like several other pubs and hotels on Point.

A famous rhyme was written about the midshipmen that frequented the hotel:
> This is the Blue Postesses, where midshipmen leave their chestesses, call for tea and toastesses, and sometimes forget to pay for their breakfastesses.

In January 1816, Madame Tussaud, the famous artist, advertised an exhibition of her unrivalled Collection of Figures as large as life, consisting of 83 Public characters, which had previously been exhibited in Paris, London, Dublin, etc. at The *Blue Posts Hotel*, Broad Street. [18]
She was fortunate to have survived the French Revolution having been imprisoned and had her hair shaved in readiness for the guillotine, before being reprieved and forced to make death masks of beheaded royals.

> In November 1800 a duel took place in a small passage (21ft x 3ft) behind the *Blue Post Tavern* between a Lieutenant Stapleton of the 20th Foot, and Ensign Grainger of the Guards, without any seconds to attend them. This duel resulted from an argument about rank on board a transport vessel at Spithead. At the due time Ensign Grainger discharged his pistol and missed,

and Lieutenant Stapleton missed fire. As a result of the missed fire, an officer's servant pricked the touch hole of Lieutenant Stapleton's pistol with a pin and then the officer fired hitting Ensign Grainger in the hip and the shot then passed into his intestines.

Lieutenant Stapleton went directly on board *The Fortitude* after the duel and was later taken to the Town gaol. In the meantime Ensign Grainger died of his wounds after 4 days. The inquest was held in the Blue Posts two days later, and the verdict was one of wilful murder, and Lieutenant Stapleton was sent to Winchester for trial.

The judge's verdict was one of manslaughter, and the sentence was 6 months imprisonment with a £50 fine, but this must have been mitigated since it was later reported that Lieutenant Stapleton was released after a period of 9 weeks. [8]

The original building was burnt down in 1870 and then rebuilt and surprisingly renamed *The Old Blue Posts*. The last owner of this famous old hotel is listed as Mrs Sarah Sharpe in 1940 and shortly afterwards the hotel suffered war damage.

The Old Blue Posts in Broad Street, pre-Second World War.

Star and Garter Hotel

Another famous Hotel situated at the northern end of Broad Street backing on to the Camber was the *Star and Garter hotel*. Although it was frequented by naval officers in particular, it was not solely confined to patronage of the Royal Navy and many famous people stayed there over the years.

These celebrity guests include Charles Dickens, William Makepeace Thackeray, Howe and Horatio Nelson, who is said to have signed his name on one of the glass windows which was later removed when the pub was demolished in the late 1950s and transferred to the Dolphin in the High Street.

William IV was a frequent visitor when he was Duke of Clarence and his regular room had a magnificent view of Portsmouth Harbour.

The deeds of the hotel stipulated that the landlord had to pay a tax of a certain number of fat capons annually, although this was later commuted to a yearly sum of money.

This hotel was widely used as an auction house, and in 1799 held an auction for materials salvaged from the East Indiaman *Henry Addington* that had been "lost" on the Bembridge Ledge off the Isle of Wight.

Other auctions of sailing vessels and materials were numerous, and regular adverts were posted in the *Hampshire Telegraph* during the nineteenth century.

The *Star and Garter* also placed adverts inviting the public to meet agents to discuss passages to France and also advertised its services for coach travel to London and other places. Adverts were also placed for auctions to be held at the hotel, such as this one below in 1802.

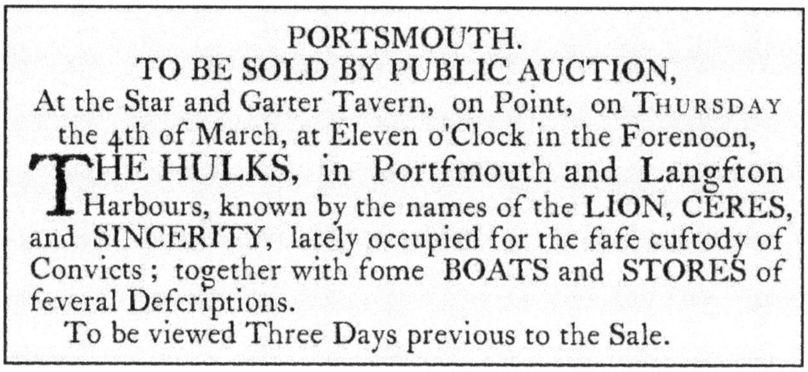

PORTSMOUTH.
TO BE SOLD BY PUBLIC AUCTION,
At the Star and Garter Tavern, on Point, on THURSDAY
the 4th of March, at Eleven o'Clock in the Forenoon,
THE HULKS, in Portfmouth and Langfton
Harbours, known by the names of the LION, CERES,
and SINCERITY, lately occupied for the fafe cuftody of
Convicts ; together with fome BOATS and STORES of
feveral Defcriptions.
To be viewed Three Days previous to the Sale.

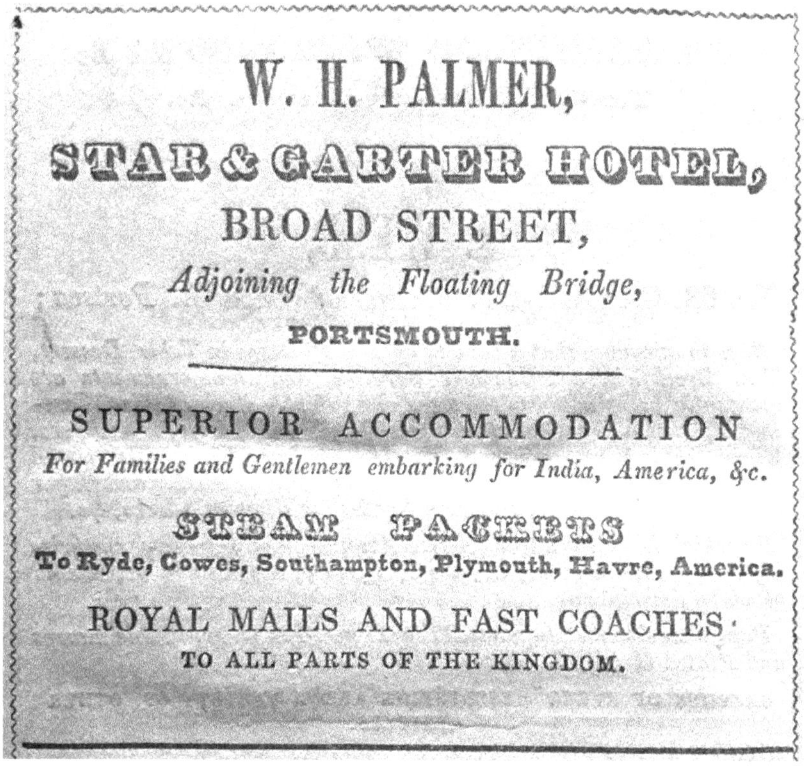

W. H. PALMER,
STAR & GARTER HOTEL,
BROAD STREET,
Adjoining the Floating Bridge,
PORTSMOUTH.

SUPERIOR ACCOMMODATION
For Families and Gentlemen embarking for India, America, &c.

STEAM PACKETS
To Ryde, Cowes, Southampton, Plymouth, Havre, America.

ROYAL MAILS AND FAST COACHES·
TO ALL PARTS OF THE KINGDOM.

An advertisement for the *Star and Garter Hotel*, advertising superior
accommodation, steam packet travel and coach transportation
to all parts of the Kingdom.

Apparently a number of Portsmouth and Portsea tradesmen formed a society called the *Portsmouth Psychrolutes* and they used to bathe on the shore near Spur Redoubt every day of the year. Christmas day was a gala day and any member not attending was fined 2/6 which the members afterwards spent on hot punch at the *Star and Garter hotel*. [19]

The *Star and Garter Hotel* in the twentieth century.

During its demolition in the late 1950s a secret room was found without a door, measuring 10ft x 6ft, and it is thought this may have been a hiding place for men trying to avoid capture by the press gangs.

Blue Anchor

The *Blue Anchor* pub at the southern end of Broad Street near the Sally Port was said to be a disreputable pub, and the following article was published in the *Hampshire Telegraph* in February 1847, just prior to the pub's demolition:-

> The low and smothering rooms put the alsatia of Sir Walter Scott in the shade: it was a perfect pandemonium; the rendezvous of the lowest of the sailors, who (thanks to the County squires and presiding Magistrates, who gave to every criminal of every grade, the option of seven years transportation or going to sea), contaminated and polluted the English navy, and degraded the bulwarks of the land to convict hulks, throwing amongst honest men, felons and the sweepings of gaols".
> To keep such fierce spirits in check, came the accursed lash on board ship, and when paid off the scenes of debauchery and brutal violence, which during the French war gave to this part of Portsmouth its fearful name.
> In the *Blue Anchor* the seamen of the *Mars* first concocted the mutiny of Spithead.
> In the tap room, the voice of the violin never was mute.

As a lad, I have been into their defiled rooms to deliver messages and parcels to the Captains and coxswains, and I have been paid bills from the apron of the landlady, held over her arm, and filled with the coinage of every part of Europe.

While the complaints were eternal to the Authorities of sailors, who in a few hours, in the buildings in the rear (a species of store, divided into sleeping rooms), had lost the whole of their pay and prize money, and from the constant influx of customers, detection was impossible.

On the first floor at the rear of the house was a regular built and formed turf cock-pit for cock fighting, where persons addicted to this species of cruelty nightly congregated, and large sums of money were lost and won!

I had lately in my possession a pair of the steel spurs which were fastened to the legs of the birds in this room and they are nearly an inch long, double edged, and as sharp as razor blades.

This was one of several pubs that were demolished c.1847 when Point Barracks were constructed.

Prince William Henry

This pub sited in West Street was named after the Prince because of an historic encounter which took place in the area. The Prince, when he was a midshipman, got into a fight in a pub with a local waterman named Billy, who was unaware of the Prince's identity when the Prince had snatched his glass of ale, taken a good drink then poured the remainder on the floor. The Prince refused to buy a replacement drink so a fight ensued at nearby Capstan Square, which was won by the waterman and the Prince was carried off by his friends in a bloodied state to the nearest apothecary for treatment.

Billy was later told who he had beaten up, and was mortified, and after hiding for a few days until he thought the storm was over, he was then summoned to attend the Admiral's house. To his surprise he wasn't punished but was offered a good job in the Customs service on the condition he never spoke of the fight. Billy kept his word and never mentioned the fight. He died aged 81 after becoming coxswain of the Customs House boat. [15]

This pub is recorded as having been demolished by 1890, and the site later became the headquarters for the Police Rowing Club.

Tower Street was another famous street for pubs on Spice Island, and one of the pubs here, the *Ship Tyger* located on the beach, had a very bad reputation.

Tower Street is referred to in several early nineteenth century Portsmouth directories as the location of numerous pubs, although it is commonly known as a short street between Tower Alley and West Street.

One explanation may be that in the 1825 Painting by Admiral Smythe, drawn from the Semaphore Tower, Tower Street appears to also run parallel to Broad Street, but to the west, from the Sally Port to the Round Tower and perhaps some of the pubs were located here. This explanation concurs with the sketch that follows of the *Fortune of War* pub, confirming its location to be in this section of Tower Street. This pub has been listed in several different Portsmouth directories as being in both Tower Street and Broad Street. It is therefore likely that it fronted both streets.

The following article was written about the *Fortune of War* and its presumed location in Tower Street is in accord with this article

In 1802 a naval officer bumped into a sailor whilst passing along a narrow passage near the *Fortune of War*, and the sailor apologised profusely. At this apology the officer drew his sword and marched the sailor firmly backwards towards the sally port from whence he had come. The sailor asked why was he pushing him back, and then he shouted for help, and the officer shouted for his ship's crew waiting on the beach.

In a moment his crew of a Midshipman and eight men were alongside him and he instructed them to seize the sailor and head for the guard-ship. On reaching the *Royal William*, the man was brought on deck and the officer said "I arrest and give into charge this man".

It turned out that the officer had been hunting the man for years, and he was one of the mutineers from the *Hermione*, who years ago had held a drawn dagger to his throat. He was the ringleader of that mutiny, named John Duncan, whose voice the officer recognised in the narrow passage.

The mutineer was subsequently hung. [20]

"The Fortune of War"

The *Fortune of War* pub sited behind the fortifications near the sally port in the centre of Eighteen gun battery. [21]

PORTSMOUTH.
TO BE SOLD BY AUCTION,

On Thursday, Feb. 25, 1802, between the Hours of Six and Eight in the Evening (unlefs fooner difpofed of by Private Contract, of which timely Notice will be given,) at the Houfe of Mr. Jofeph Smith, bearing the fign of the Sun, near the Point Gates,

 THE good Carvel-built Cutter, called the ANT, burthen about 32 Tons per regifter.

The above veffel is well found, fails remarkably well, would make an excellent Packet or Pleafure Yacht, having good accommadations. She is at present employed as a Paffage Veffel, between Portfmouth and Plymouth.

For Inventory and Particulars, apply to Mr. Craves, 147, Queen- freet, Portfea.

PORTSMOUTH,
TO BE SOLD BY PRIVATE CONTRACT,

 THE following VESSELS, viz, the faft-failing Smack FRIENDS, burthen forty-three tons per regifter, built at Cowes, one-year old; the faid Smack is bullwark'd all round, and ready for Sea without any further expenfe.

Alfo, the good Smack DANIEL, burthen 25 tons, built at Cowes, is eight years old, and now employed as a Paffage Veffel between Portfmouth and Plymouth.

For further particulars apply Mr. Richard Hafkell, at the fign of the Thatched Houfe on the Point, where an Inventory of each Veffels' Materials may be had.

The above adverts show that many pubs on Point were used for auctions and sales, as these adverts show for the *Sun* and the *Thatched House*.

East Street also had numerous pubs and taverns in an area where many poor people lived in very close quarters, like several other areas on Point. Some of these pubs were on the Town Quay and one pub, the *Orange Tree Tavern*, overlooked the Inner Camber. It used to have a skittle alley at its rear and it was a very popular place and its remarkably fine ballroom was celebrated for its social functions. The pub was finally demolished in 1913 together with old houses and stores to make way for the Town Quay improvements.

Sometimes, serious acts of violence occurred in pubs as written in the following report:

> In 1735 on the return of *HMS Centurion* to Portsmouth with the Admirals dispatches the crew were given shore leave and went ashore at the Point where there were many other sailors from ships in port, some with pockets full of prize money.
> A public house in East Street was noted for its attractive women, over whom quarrels often sprung up as suddenly as a squall.
> In one of those brawls a foreign sailor in a fit of jealousy unsheathed his clasp knife, seeking with tigerish animosity to wreak vengeance on a rival.
> His ferocity was short lived. A fierce scuffle ensued and screams of "murder" resounded in East Street.
> The naval patrols were non-existent in those days, order being kept, except when Press gangs were busy, by "watchmen".
> The foreign sailor's maltreated body was evidently smuggled away, but its destination was never discovered; and indeed remained a mystery till the mid nineteenth century when the public house was demolished.
> Bricked up in the old fashioned chimney nook was found the skeleton of the murdered man. The bones were decently interred, without an antiquarian inquest being held by the considerate medico who was Borough Coroner at that time. [4]

Trouble sometimes broke out during "runs ashore" and in one incident in March 1750 it was reported that 200 sailors armed with clubs went to the back of the Point to a public house which they almost pulled down. They threw the beds and furniture about the street and stove all the beer in the cellars, after which they came into town and went into several public houses, broke the windows, stove the butts of beer and inflicted other considerable damage.

The following articles appeared in the local newspaper about publicans on the Point.

> A few days since a publican at Portsmouth being willing to try what hanging was, tied himself up with a cord, and at the same time held a sharp knife in his hand, in order to cut himself down, but, missing the rope, he cut his throat quite through the windpipe, in which shocking situation he was found: he is supposed to have died worth near £8,000. (July 1765)

> On Monday last a man that keeps a house of ill fame on the back of the Point, struck a seaman on the head with the bar of the door and fractured his skull. The seaman wanted to come into the publican's house; some words arose, when the barbarous fellow made use of the above weapon, which was fit to knock down an ox. The publican has absconded; the man was sent to Haslar hospital, but expired the next day. (February 1772)

Publicans on Point had a somewhat notorious reputation as this description from one visitor to Portsmouth in 1805 attests:

> There is nothing a Portsmouth publican likes to handle like, as it is called, a fresh gurnet with a pudding in his belly; meaning a sailor who has just received his pay and has more cash in his pocket than wit to his sconce; they are never off their guard and their fingers are always itching to be in your purse. They have no idea of generosity, and you may as well look for a magpie in

the moon, or fish in a fresh river for a salt herring, as to expect liberality in a Portsmouth publican. [22]

Throughout its history Point had at least two breweries and many beer houses.
The first mention of a brewery is of one set up and operated by a William Norris in 1759. Subsequent to this the Fountain Brewery was located at 6 East Street between 1807 and 1865. This brewery was set up by Joseph Knott on land made available when the Camber Dock was reconstructed. He owned a couple of public houses and continued brewing until his death in 1850. [86]

The centre of the Portsmouth brewing industry was located close to the Point in Penny Street, where there were at one time three breweries in operation:
Between 1695 and 1843 a brewery operated here by Messrs Mudge & Deacon, and from 1719 to 1910 there was a brewery operated by Messrs Pike & Carter and between 1770 to 1902 *The Portsmouth brewery* operated here by Messrs Norris & Garrett.
All these breweries relied on horse drawn drays to deliver the beer and of the five breweries existing in Portsmouth in 1784 the three largest were those in Penny Street. [23]

In the eighteenth and nineteenth centuries, coffee houses at the Point were used as auction houses for the sale of prize vessels. Some of the pubs also fulfilled this function, including the *Isle of Wight Hoy*, in addition to holding bankruptcy hearings. Auctions of vessels are recorded in the *Hampshire Telegraph* as taking place in the late eighteenth and early nineteenth century in the *Kings Head*, *Star and Garter*, *Thatched House* and the *Sun*.
These vessels and their marine gear were often substantial vessels with some recorded as being in excess of 100 tons.

In addition to the large pubs where the role of water transportation and coach travel has been outlined, a significant number of the smaller Broad Street pubs on Point were also involved in arranging transportation by water. The abundance of these journeys by road and water demonstrates how busy the Point must have been.

Several pubs were demolished in 1847 in advance of the construction of Point Barracks on the west side of Broad Street between the Sally Port and the Round Tower.
In 1846 the Board of Ordnance purchased 19 properties in Broad Street, and in February 1847 the materials were sold off and demolition started shortly after this sale (The sum realised for the sale of materials was only £556).
At least 8 pubs were demolished in Broad Street including the *Queen's Head* (ex *Lord Hood and General Elliot*), *Bridge Tavern*, *Three Guns*, *Blue Anchor*, *Dorsetshire Tavern* (ex. *Prince of Wales*), *Vine*, *Sun* and the *Fortune of War*. Probably the most famous name among these was the *Blue Anchor* which was apparently purchased for £31 in the sale with the purchaser having already sold the lead on the roof for £30.

The new Barracks included a guard house, accommodation for a detachment of artillery and a depot for stores and ammunition.

Some drinking establishments were of a much higher standard than others; - the coaching inns were among the best, with the well-established pubs being of a reasonable standard and beer houses being at the lower end of the scale. [24]
Unfortunately, the drinking of beer became very much a family way of life and working class women in particular, turned to the demon drink whilst their husbands were away at sea. The living conditions of many of the working class inhabitants of Spice Island were very poor and

beer houses provided a brief respite from this way of life. As a result of this drinking, it was not unusual to see many drunks on the street and people lying asleep in the gutters.

Because of this antisocial behaviour, people started campaigning to have changes made to the status quo and in the late nineteenth century temperance campaigners appeared. In time this started to have an effect on drinking habits as pub's licensing hours started being restricted following their "open all hours" culture that had existed for many years. By 1872 a law came into force that pubs had to close by 11pm, but because there were so many drinking establishments available late drinking still went on. [15]

The number of pubs on Spice Island started to dwindle in the mid to late nineteenth century with the expansion of Portsmouth and its Naval Dockyard, and the change from sail to steam driven ships.

This resulted in far fewer licenced watermen over time and many of the historical trades and shops on Spice Island including sailmakers and slop sellers, among others, started to diminish.

The reduction in the demand for pubs continued throughout the early twentieth century, exacerbated by the loss of some residential housing in the area, which was demolished as being unfit for human habitation. Furthermore, some pubs were lost, following demolition, as a result of expansion and improvements to the Town Quay and adjacent area.

Further damage was done to the area during World War 2 and today there are only three pubs remaining: the *Bridge Tavern* in East Street on the Town Quay, the *Still and West* in Bath Square and the *Spice Island Inn* on the Point which was formed by the amalgamation of the *Lone Yachtsman* (formerly the *Union Tavern*) and the *Coal Exchange* in 1991.

These are all very popular pubs, especially during the summer months when their trade is greater, fuelled by tourists and other visitors to Portsmouth.

The Point is such a different place today compared to yesteryear with far less industry and many more residential properties and of course the visiting mariners from around the globe have gone, being replaced by other visitors and tourists.
The modern day way of life has fuelled the demise of pubs, but it is incredible to think that two or three centuries ago there were 40 to 50 pubs on Point!
A visit to Point in those days would have been something to behold!

Notes

An attempt has been made in this book to tabulate all the known pubs that have existed on Point since the area was inhabited and kind thanks are given to Stephen Pomeroy for the extensive data published on his website. Dates included are the earliest known reference dates for the pubs, but in many cases the pubs may have existed before that date. It does however, give a good idea of most of the pubs that have existed on Point throughout the centuries. [25]

The exact locations of some of the earlier pubs are unknown, since historical information lists them as being on "the Beach" or on "the Point (Poynt)" which is often a reference to the whole area of Spice Island

The street numbering system in Broad Street changed sometime between 1865 and 1870. The numbering prior to this originally commenced consecutively from No. 1 on the east side next to King James's Gate heading northwards towards the Point, and then continued southwards on the west side of Broad Street up to the Sally Port where the last property was No. 98 (the Sun public house) prior to its demolition circa 1847. Numbering today consists of even numbers on the east side and odd numbers on the west side.

It should be noted that some of the pubs changed their names throughout history, and in some instances more than once, and sometimes more than two pubs existed with the same name.

LIST OF PUBS BY STREET

Broad Street

1. *Arathusa*, 1823, (latterly listed as *Royal Marine, Arathusa and Circe, the Arethusa, Circe and Arethusa*) 3/8 Broad Street.

2. *Berwick and Nonsuch*, 1784.

3. *Black Swan*, 1716, 23/56 Broad Street.

4. *Blue Anchor*, 1784, (latterly the *Crown*), 95 Broad Street.

5. *Blue Posts Tavern*, 1613, (*Two Blue Posts, Blew Post, The Blue Posts Inn, Blue Posts Tavern and Hotel, Blue Posts Hotel, Old Blue Posts*) 18/38 Broad Street.

6. *Bridge Tavern*, 1844, 92 Broad Street.

7. *Cornish Arms*, 1798, (*Cornish Arms Tavern, Prussian Eagle*), 71/9 Broad Street.

8. *Crown*, 1716, Broad Street east side.

9. *Dun cow*, 1687.

10-. *Fortitude*, 1786, (*Fortitude Tavern*), 49/53 Broad Street, but also fronted Bath Square.

11. *Fortune of War*, 1716, 94 Broad Street, also mentioned as being located in Tower Street.

12. *Fountain Tavern*, 1784, Broad Street, east side.

13. *Golden Cross, (Lion and Lamb)*, 75/76 Broad Street.

14. *Isle of Man*, 1823, 71 Broad Street.

15. *King of Prussia*, 1784, 12 Broad Street.

16. *King's Arms*, 1784, (*King's Arms Tavern*), 35/80 Broad Street.

17. *King's Head Tavern*, 1652, (*Somerset Tavern, Somerset Hotel*), 40/92 Broad Street.

18. *Lion,* 1607, (possibly *White Lyon* near King James's Gate, or *White Lion* in Broad Street, east side.

19. *London*, 1716, Broad Street, west side.

20. *Lord Hood and General Elliot*, 1784, (*Queen's Head*), 87 Broad Street.

21. *Madras Tavern*.

22. *Navy Tavern*, 1784.

23. *Neptune and Mars*, 1784, 55/41 Broad Street, with alley to Bath Square.

24. *Neptune's Court*, 1676.

25. *Old King of Prussia*, 1784.

26. *Old Point Tavern*.

27. *Peabody's vat* 1802, (Initially a beer retailer, then latterly *The Seagull),* 13 Broad Street.

28. *Plymouth Trader*, 1784, (*Victoria, Victoria Tavern*), 46 Broad Street.

29. *Portland Arms,* 1847.

30. *Prince of Wales*, 1784, (latterly *Royal George, Dorsetshire Tavern*), 96 Broad Street.

31. *Queen Charlotte*, 1823, 41 Broad Street.

32. *Roebuck*, 1712, (*Roebuck Tavern*) 52/45 Broad Street, (also fronted on to 13 Bath Square)

33. *Romney*, 1784.

34. *Royal George*, 1823, 2 Broad Street.

35. *St Alban's*, 1784, (*The Ship St Alban's, Sunderland Arms*) 39 Broad Street.

36. *St George*, 1612, (*The George, Plume of Feathers, Cap and Feathers, New Chatham, Coach and Horses*) 74/3 Broad Street.

37. *Sloop,* 1784.

38. *Southampton Hoy*, 1716.

39. *Star and Garter Tavern*, 1784, (*Star and Garter Hotel*), 43/100 Broad Street.

40. *Sun,* 1644, 98 Broad Street.

41. *Thatched House*, 1784, 53 Broad Street.

42. *Three Guns*, 1784, 93 Broad Street.

43. *True Blue*, 1823, 37 Broad Street.

44. *The Union*, 1715, *(Union Tavern, Union Jack, Lone Yachtsman)*, 65 Broad Street.

45. *Vine,* 1784, 97 Broad Street.

46. *White Hart*, 1676, (*White Hart Tavern*), Broad Street east side.

47. *White Swan*, 1784, 54/43 Broad Street.

48. *Worcester*, 1784, (*Ship Worcester*), 42/98 Broad Street.

East Street

1. *Anchor and Crown*, 1784, (latterly *Crown and Anchor)*

2. *Anchor*, 1851, 21 East Street.

3. *Bridge Tavern*, 1844, 54 East Street.

4. *Butcher's Arms*, 1863, (*Camber House, Camber Cellars*) 27 East Street.

5. *Collier's Arms*, 1887, East Street, north quay.

6. *Globe,* 1682, (Smocke Alley), East Street.

7. *King William*, 1851, East Street south side.

8. *Lamb and Flag*, 1784, East Street north side.

9. *Nelson's Arms*, 1830.

10. *North Country Pink*, 1784, (*Sunderland Pink, Olive Branch, Olive Branch Tavern, The Ellington*) 29 East Street.

11. *Orange Tree*, 1694, (*Orange Tree Tavern*) 24 East Street.

12. *Queen's Head*, 1654.

13. *Sir Charles Napier*, 1851, beer retailer? 10 East Street.

14. *Three Tuns*, 1784, (*Three Tuns Tavern, Shoveller's Arms*), 40 East Street.

15. *Vine*, 1784.

16. *William the Fourth*, 1853, beer retailer? 28 East Street.

Bath Square

1. *East and West Country House*, 1839, (*Rose & Crown Inn, West Country House*), 3 or 5 Bath Square.

2. *Fortitude Tap,* (rear of *Fortitude Tavern*), 1865, 7 Bath Square.

3. *Isle of Wight Hoy*, 1702, (*Ile of Wite hige, Isle of Wight Sloop, Isle of Wight Tavern*), 1865, Bath Square.

4. *New York Tavern*, 1847, 13 Bath Square.

5. *North Country*, 1830, (*North Country Tavern and Coal Exchange, North Country House Tavern, Jolly Sailor, Coal Exchange, Spice Island Inn*), 1 Bath Square.

6. *Rose and Crown*, 1716.

7. *Roving Sailor*

8. *Still,* 1733, (*Still Tavern, Still and West Country House*)

9. *Three Horseshoes*, 1823.

10. *West Country House*, 1839, (*East and West Country House*)

11. *West India Tavern*, 1754, (*The Quebec Hotel, West India and Quebec Tavern, Quebec Hotel*)

Tower Street

1. *Black Horse,* 1823, (*Black Horse Tavern*)

2. *Cock and Pigeon*, 1776, (*Jolly Waterman*).

3. *Dolphin*, 1715.

4. *Lord Hood,* 1823, Tower Street/Capstan Square.

5. *Plough,* 1784.

6. *Plymouth Arms,* 1716, (*Old Plymouth Arms*).

7.   *Sun*, 1784.

8.   *Tyger*, 1784, (*Ship Tyger, Ship Tiger*).

West Street

1.   *Pack Horse*, 1784, (*Old Pack Horse*).

2.   *Prince William*, 1784, (*Prince William Henry*).

3.   *Robin Hood and Little John*, 1784.

Point

1.   *Bell*, 1716.

2.   *Black Dog*, 1728.

3.   *Bricklayer's Arms*, 1716.

4.   *Circe,* 1800.

5.   *Cross Keys*, 1716.

6.   *Crown,* 1716.

7.   *Earl Howe*, 1784.

8.   *Fishing Hoy*, 1716.

9.   *Five Bells*, 1716.

10.   *Golden Hart*, 1828.

11.   *Greyhound and Last*, 1716.

12.   *Guernsey*, 18th century.

13.   *King George's Head*, 1716.

14.   *Last*, 1716.

15.   *London*, 1656.

16.   *Nors Toy,* 1716.

17.   *Old Plough*, 1784.

18.   *Redcraft,* 1669.

19.   *Rose and Crown*, 1716.

20.   *Row Barge*, 1716.

21.   *Scotch Cross,* 1684.

22.   *Seven Stars*, 1716.

23.   *Thistle and Crown*, 1715 on the beach.

24.   *Three Golden Pots*, 1784, on the beach.

25.   *Three Guns Inn*, 1716 (*Ordnance Arms*).

26.   *Three Kings*, 1784.

Chapter 5

Press Gangs (The Impress Service)

The Royal Navy has always had problems recruiting personnel to crew their ships, particularly in times of war. The practice of forcing men to serve in the navy is as old as our naval records and as early as 1206 the King's ships were usually manned by impressment.

Samuel Pepys, reflecting on the scenes of impressment that came to his notice in June 1666 wrote:

> But Lord! How some poor women did cry and in my life I never did see such natural expression of passion as I did here, in some women's bewailing themselves and running to every parcel of men that were brought, one after another, to look for their husbands, and wept over every vessel that went off, thinking they might be there, and looking after the ship as far as ever they could by moonlight, that it grieved me to the heart to hear them. Besides, to see poor patient labouring men and housekeepers leaving poor wives and families taken up on a sudden by strangers was very hard, and that without press money, but forced against all law to be gone. It is a great tyranny. [5]

The system of pressing people into the service was despised by many and a Doctor Trotter, a naval surgeon on a receiving ship, wrote in 1819 that:

> The scenes of cruelty and affliction which have come under my review have wrung my heart a thousand times. They are not fit to be related here, or indeed, anywhere else, for they exhibit all that is ferocious in the business of war, and disgusting and deformed in the policy of a country that can permit the practice to be continued.

It was commented on by many to be the equivalent of "white slavery."

As Portsmouth grew as a naval town, the press gangs became a common feature in the old town and the Impress Service was in full swing towards the close of the eighteenth century, continuing until the end of the Great War.

There were three methods of recruiting naval personnel: voluntary service, impressment and (from 1795)-Quota Acts.

Volunteers for the Royal Navy would receive conduct money and two months wages in advance, from which clothes and a hammock, known as slops had to be purchased from the Purser.

Not all those classified as volunteers volunteered willingly, since often a man taken by the press gang would be offered the chance to volunteer and so receive the bounty and he would then be entered on the muster book as- 'V' instead of 'P' for pressed.

"Gala Press Gang 1798" by F. J. Proctor. This painting shows a scene in Portsmouth near the Square Tower, with the bust of Charles I clearly visible. It shows the press gang in operation rounding up men to be pressed into service with their loved ones bitterly trying to prevent this happening. © Portsmouth Museum Service.

At times of war there was always a shortage of trained sailors and although untrained men could be used to pull ropes, manhandle guns etc., only a trained man could be capable of working aloft 30 to 40 feet above the deck.

The figures below indicate the number of seaman and marines serving in the English Navy:-

1793.	1794.	1797.	1800
45,000.	85,000.	120,000.	130,000.

In 1804 Parliament voted for 100,000 men to be recruited to the navy but only 84,000 were actually recruited. In the following year it voted for 120,000 and only got 109,000.
When the Napoleonic Wars began in 1803 the British Navy was near the peak of its power and each British Admiral was expected to annihilate the enemy.
In the wars of 1793 to 1808 the British Navy fought 5 fleet battles defeating the French (twice), the Dutch, Spanish and Danes. [26]

The navy was made up from seamen from many nations, including Ireland, as well as black recruits from the West Indies and the Americas.

The Press or Impress Service used to send out gangs of 8 to 12 men with an officer to locate anyone between the ages of 18 and 55, ideally with sea experience, and try to persuade them to join. Very few would join voluntarily so they were "pressed" into the Navy Service.

The officers serving the warrants were given strict instructions not to impress or (if impressed) detain any Masters of merchant ships or vessels; or the First Mates, Boatswains, or Carpenters of such as are of 50 tons or upwards; persons above 55 or under 18 years of age, foreigners, apprentices and all other persons belonging to vessels in the immediate or constant employ of the Public Offices (Navy, Victualling, Ordnance, Customs, Excise, Post Office).

They were often treated very badly to get them aboard: common tactics included threatening with pistol and musket, physical violence and plying the recruits with alcohol.

The recruits were offered the King's shilling as a bounty for joining. Sometimes a shilling would be slipped into the pocket or tankard of ale, which is why landlords later used glass bottom tankards.

Seamen from Merchant ships were generally thought more valuable than other pressed men and were sometimes "pressed" into service, although officers were exempt. Apprentices with less than 2 years' experience were also exempt as a result of their highly sought after exemption "tickets."

"The Neglected Tar" by Unknown artist © National Maritime Museum, Greenwich, London depicting a scene showing a husband and father being unwillingly dragged off to sea by a press gang.

Merchant Navy pay was far better than the Royal Navy and was approximately four times more.
Another source of seamen after the start of the Napoleonic Wars was to press men who were returning home after being returned by the French in exchange for French prisoners.

Due to shortages of men available to the Royal Navy, Parliament passed the Quota Acts in 1795 which required each County to produce a quota of men, depending on its population and number of ports.
Initially, a very high bounty of £5 was offered to an able seaman, £4 to an ordinary seaman and £3 to a landsman, together with conduct money (travelling expenses) from the place of abode but this soon increased as men became harder to find. To incentivise volunteers, Justices of the Peace would reduce convicts' sentences if they "volunteered" for the navy, or would offer criminals a choice between jail or navy, at their trials.

As recruiting became more difficult, very high bounties were offered, sometimes as high as £30 for an individual man. This resulted in all the disreputable people from the counties joining the navy and it is noteworthy that some of the later mutineers were recruited this way.

A pressed man was in the navy until the end of the war and the wars with the French lasted for 22 years. As it became more and more difficult to find seaman, as was the case in 1803, permission was given for press gangs to press from "protections" and to take anyone connected with the sea.

There were some real battles with the press gangs as locals often stood together and formed armed gangs to protect their men; indeed there were instances of fatalities arising from the process of impressing men for the service.

"The Liberty of the Subject (Press gang)" by James Gillray 1779 © National Maritime Museum, Greenwich, London.

In past times Point was an island, and there was a moat or ditch across what is now Broad Street in front of St James's Gate, which extended from the sea on the west side, into the Camber on the other. It was also possible to swim ashore near the Sally Port and under the bridge by King James's gate arriving in the Camber.

To gain access to and from Point one had to cross an ordinary drawbridge and it was at the Sally Port near King James's Gate that the press gangs often landed at night, on many occasions rushing into Point across the drawbridge where they captured scores of unfortunate victims. It was well known that some of the pubs on Spice Island had hiding places for men being pursued by the press gangs and tales are told of men that had been pressed into service jumping into the sea as the boat left the harbour, swimming ashore to be hidden in one of the local pubs until the coast was clear - all for a fee, of course!

On one occasion crowds were lined up in Bath Square to watch the departure of a British man-of war for Foreign Service: as she passed by a sailor jumped overboard, landed near the Round Tower and rushed up Capstan Square before disappearing down Tower Alley into Broad Street.

He was soon lost in the crowds, but ultimately his destination was mooted among the natives as a public house of eminent propriety, whose landlord could be squared by a deserter because he himself was adept at bribing inquisitive officials. When this public house was searched by the naval police the sailor would hide in a secret room on the top floor, the entrance to which was effected by sliding aside a panel.

When the coast was clear the sailor would emerge and pay up for the help given to avoid a foreign commission of 5 to 7 years. [4]

The document below is an example of a Press Warrant issued to a ship's captain in 1809:

By the Commissioners for Executing the Office
of Lord High Admiral of the United Kingdom
of *Great Britain* and *Ireland, &c.* and of all
His Majesty's Plantations, &c.

IN Pursuance of His Majesty's Order in Council, dated the Sixteenth Day of *November*, 1804, We do hereby Impower and Direct you to impress, or cause to be impressed, so many Seamen, Seafaring Men and Persons whose Occupations and Callings are to work in Vessels and Boats upon Rivers, as shall be neccesary either to Man His Majesty's Ship under your Command or any other of His Majesty's Ships, giving unto each Man so impressed One Shilling for Prest Money. And in the execution hereof, you are to take care that neither yourself nor any Officer authorised by you do demand or receive any Money, Gratuity, Reward or other Consideration whatsoever, for the sparing, Exchanging or Discharging any Person or Persons impressed or to be impressed as you will answer to it at your Peril. You are not to intrust any Person with the execution of this Warrant, but a Commission Officer and to insert his Name and Office in the Deputation on the other side hereof, and set your Hand and Seal thereto. --- This Warrant to continue in Force til the Thirty First Day of December 1809, and in the due execution thereof, all Mayors, Sherrifs, Justices of the Peace, Bailiffs, Constables Headboroughs, and all other His Majesty's Officers and Subjects whom it may concern, are hereby required to be aiding and assisting unto you, and those employed by you, as they tender His Majesty's Service, and will answer the contrary at their Perils.

Given under our Hands and the Seal of the Office of Admiralty, the   1809.

Captain
Commander of His Majesty's
the
    By Command of their Lordships,

The press gang were a constant source of terror in seaport towns like Portsmouth, but in times of peace there was no need to impress seamen.

> Merchant seamen coming home from long and tedious voyages for relaxation, were seized in the Channel, at the Nore, or St Helen's, dragged into tenders and hurried off without seeing home of friends, for five or six years more of compulsory misery and privation. Slavery itself was not more iniquitous and oppressive and the press inspired terror in all classes; tailors and other workmen dressed in female garb and carried the produce of their labour home to their employers by stealth and in darkness. [16]

Merchant seamen were stowed away in horrid holes for weeks at a time and were on occasion, dragged from their hiding places with violence, sometimes sustaining dreadful wounds. Furthermore, constables and peace officers promising them security for a financial sum, not infrequently betrayed their trust and handed them over to their oppressors.
It was well-known that these pressed men cursed their fate and hated the service; indeed pressed men were the most mutinous - the most prominent among the Nore and Spithead mutineers all being pressed men.

The *Hampshire Telegraph* records that at the beginning of the seventeenth century there was an agency in Portsmouth devoted to the supply of substitutes for pressed men. The average price of a substitute was about 10 guineas, although how much of that went to the seaman and how much remained in the pockets of the agent, history does not record.

The most active period of the press gang in Portsmouth appears to have been in 1803, which marked the beginning of the final struggle between England and Napoleon and in March of that year the press gang scoured the streets and even broke into private houses in search of men they suspected to be in concealment there.

> On March 14th 1803 a very hot press occurred on Tuesday night, at this place and the neighbourhood, by which 500 able seamen were obtained.
> It was chiefly planned and conducted by Captain Bowen who pressed a great number of seamen and able watermen by the following strategy:
> At 10 o'clock at night he assembled a party of marines with as much noise and parade as possible to quell a pretended riot at Fort Monckton in Gosport. As the news spread, everybody ran to the Fort and when Capt. Bowen saw he had attained his objective he silently placed a party of marines at the end of Haslar Bridge, next to the Hospital, and took every man that answered his purpose as he returned from the scene of the false alarm. [8])

This is the only instance on record of any great number of useful men being obtained locally in one press; it was usually the very opposite and the misery, the terror and the disgust produced in all classes of society by impressment, was never compensated for by the very few good men added to the service through its instrumentality.
Also, in March of that year frigates and gunboats were dispatched from Portsmouth to Jersey and Guernsey on this secret service of impressment and twelve recruiting parties, with impress warrants, were appointed to accompany them. Similar orders were sent to the commanding officers of the Plymouth and Chatham divisions.

Frequently, when seamen were scarce, large towns such as Portsmouth offered bounties of their own.
On May 19th 1803 an advertisement appeared in the *Hampshire Telegraph* offering an additional sum for those entering the navy:

BOROUGH OF PORTESMOUTH.

ADDITIONAL BOUNTY TO SEAMEN.

THE CORPORATION of PORTSMOUTH having refolved to give TWENTY SHILLINGS, in addition to his Majefty's Royal Bounty, to each of the firft Hundred ABLE SEAMEN who fhall enter into his Majefty's Navy at this Place; all ABLE SEAMEN are hereby invited to come forward and apply to Mr. LUSCOMBE, one of the Town Serjeants, when, if approved of, they will be entitled to the the above Bounty, which will be paid to them immediately on their entering.

And as a further encouragement, Admiral Lord Gardner, has confented, that they fhall be at liberty to enter on board of any of his Majefty's Ships at this Port, as are not already manned.   ROGER CALLAWAY, Town Clerk.

May 19, 1803.

The following reports were commonplace, describing acts of impressment at the beginning of The nineteenth century:

> The "Press" continues very active in Portsmouth, large parties of seamen, about 600, were ordered on shore in separate gangs last night, and so peremptory were they, that they indiscriminately took out every man on board the colliers, etc. Early this morning, the same bustle was repeated, and several gangs paraded Point, and picked up many useful hands, and lodged them in the guard house on the Grand Parade. [27]

> Last evening at 8 o'clock, a very hot press took place in Portsmouth, Portsea and Gosport, in the Harbour, and most places in the neighbourhood; no protestations were listened to, and a vast number of persons of various descriptions were sent on board the different ships in this port, most of whom were this morning liberated, being master tradesmen, apprentices, and such persons; very few were detained in comparison with the number taken on board. On the whole it is not supposed the service has acquired 50 serviceable men. [28]

There were some serious "pressing" events that ended in fatalities and one of these was recounted in a London newspaper in April 1803:

> A terrible affair happened on Saturday night. A press gang from the *L'Aigle* frigate lying in Portland Roads, consisting of Captain Wolfe and his Lieutenant, with a Lieutenant of Marines, 27 Marines and about as many sailors, came on shore at Portland Castle, and proceeded to the first village, called Cheselton.
> They impressed Henry Wiggott and Richard Way without any interruption whatever. The people of the island then took alarm, and fled to the village of Eason, situated about the centre of the island, where they made a stand at the pond.
> The gang came up, and the Captain took a man by the collar. The man pulled back, on which the Captain fired his pistol, at which signal the Lieutenant of Marines ordered his men to fire, which

being done, three men fell dead, being all shot through the head, all married men, two quarrymen and one blacksmith. One man was shot through the thigh, and a young woman in the back; the ball is still in her body, and little hopes are entertained for her recovery. The poor blacksmith was at his doorstep when he fell dead.

This article caused a sensation at the time, forcing the navy to make a statement which was most unusual. They gave a different account, stating that they had been fired on and the case was afterwards subject to criminal proceedings. Although the Lieutenant and Master's mate were fully committed to Dorchester for murder and the evidence made clear that the naval party had acted with needless violence, the whole affair was smoothed over, and Captain Wolfe gained credit for the vigour with which he enforced his Press warrants."

A further case occurred in March 1800 when a midshipman killed a man during an impressment operation. This officer was subsequently acquitted on producing their Press Warrants.

Impressment was last used in Britain during the Napoleonic Wars of 1803-1815, and although it was never enforced after that period, the right to use impressment was retained. In 1835 a statute was passed that exempted sailors who had been impressed and had served for five years in the navy from any further impressment. In 1853 the navy introduced continuous service for sailors who wished to make a career in the navy and after a fixed number of years they would receive a pension. This reduced the need for general impressment and it died out in the form that it had been used previously. [29]

Portsmouth Point experienced numerous press gang activities during the period that impressment was carried out in the country. Being the home of the Royal Navy it was predictable that crew for the navy would be sought here by press gangs, since the Point offered all the 'facilities' that sailors would want on returning home after a voyage away.

Chapter 6

Flooding and Storm Damage

Spice Island has always suffered from tidal flooding, usually occurring when a combination of high spring tides and severe weather conditions occur together.

This combination of predicted high tides, low pressure and strong winds from the southern quarter, results in a tidal surge which, when added to the predicted high tide and wind-driven waves, causes flooding and often severe damage to properties and sea defences. This has occurred on a regular basis on Spice Island for many years due to its low lying nature, and until recently, its lack of adequate tidal defences.

From the time this shingle spit was first inhabited at the end of the sixteenth/beginning of the seventeenth century, flooding has been an accepted way of life and residents have dealt with it in various ways.

As development progressed on Spice Island, more and more people were squeezed into the area, resulting in deteriorating living conditions for many. These conditions became very unsanitary for those living in the area. During some very high spring tides the Point boys could row their boats in Broad Street beyond King James's gate and their punts up the High Street, through Oyster Street and even Golden Lion Lane and Lombard Street, across the Town Quay to the swollen Camber. [4] There is no record of flooding this severe in the past century.

During these high tides and the resultant flooding, it doesn't bear thinking about what was floating in the flood water. In the mid nineteenth century there were open sewers in the area, and animals, both pets and livestock, ran amok in the streets, creating an environment that was far from hygienic. Since the cellars of properties flooded on a regular basis, this must have resulted in extremely undesirable living conditions for the poorer residents, with serious illnesses occurring due to these unhealthy conditions.

The following flooding and storm damage accounts from the late eighteenth/ early nineteenth centuries give an idea of the severity of these events:

> On February 1st 1775 there was a great storm and floods in Portsmouth and a whole row of houses at the back of the Point were swept away, but no lives were lost. Other portions of Portsea Island were also under water and hundreds of sheep and cattle were drowned. [5]
>
> On Monday 21st November 1808 it was recorded that the tide flowed higher here yesterday than it has done for these six years. It came three parts of the way up Broad Street and small boats navigated up to the Blue Posts. Several shops at the lower end of the street had 30 inches

of water in them and several persons sustained considerable damage. It has not flowed to such a great height but twice, since about thirty years, when the tide was nine inches higher than was ever remembered before. The wind was blowing a tremendous gale from the south, at the full of the moon, is the cause of it. [8]

In addition to the former, several other severe flooding events were reported in the *Hampshire Telegraph* in the early nineteenth century.

On Wednesday last on March 4th 1818 at about 5 o'clock a gale of wind commenced here from the southward, which by its violence approached nearly to a hurricane.
It acted with such irresistible power upon the sea that the tide rose five feet higher than the ordinary spring tides and maintained that height three hours after it should have ebbed: it was high water between nine and ten, and so continued until midnight, and by passing and destroying its accustomed bounds (in some parts to full half a mile extent) property to a vast amount was destroyed.

The buildings between the Round Tower and the Point, are either in ruins, washed away, or their foundations undermined: the water was two feet above the pavement in Point street: the damage done to property in the cellars and lower rooms was very great.

Several small buildings next to the harbour's mouth were washed away, together with the steps at the Sally Ports and their platforms. The Slaughter-house Wharf was much damaged and many other parts of Portsea Island were inundated with water. [30]

Furthermore, when the storm of March 4th 1818 subsided a perfect skeleton was found beneath the Round Tower. It was believed to be that of a marine who was murdered in 1780 by a woman named Baker and her daughter with whom he cohabited. [5]

Yesterday we experienced the most tremendous gale of wind from the SSE that has occurred for many years, the sea ran to an extraordinary height, but the ships of war and numerous wind bound merchantmen sustained no injury. The tide rose to a considerable height in the harbour - flooded the lower part of the houses on the Point and burst through all the principal sewers of the town. [31]

On Monday November 29th 1824 a report was written in the *Hampshire Telegraph* about the dreadful hurricanes that had prevailed for the last week. The report gave great detail of the havoc caused in Plymouth and of a rescue of the crew of a vessel that ran aground at Gilkicker Point. With regards Point, the following comments were written:

Some houses on the Point were much shook, and had the tide flowed to its usual calculated period that portion called Bath Square must have been levelled, but the wind having at noon shifted about 4 points to the WSW, the tide was checked from flowing into the harbour by more than an hour's rise. The sea flowed over the whole length of the Southsea Common.

This comment about the wind shifting to the west shortly before high water averting severe flood damage is a phenomenon that has occurred on numerous occasions that I have personally witnessed over the years.

The alleged highest flooding event occurred on Spice Island on November 15th 1840 with a recorded height of 5.90 metres above Chart Datum (although the newspaper report of this event suggested a higher tide some years previous).

It is difficult to be certain of the accuracy of this measurement as the Portsmouth tide gauge was only installed in 1831 in the Naval Base, but it is reported that this was the highest tide experienced in living memory at that time.

The event was reported in the *Hampshire Telegraph* on November 16th:

> An awfully grand expression of the Divine might was manifested here yesterday by a severe gale of wind accompanied by a rise of tide, higher than had been known for 38 years, by at least an inch and a half, as recorded by an inhabitant of Point who notches his door post as an unerring proof. Although the weather was severe, most vessels held their anchoring positions at Spithead but one vessel was driven ashore at Haslar and another was beached on Southsea beach.

The following comments were made about the Point:

> Though the Point is much exposed, little comparative damage was done. The back part of a small but old house in Tower Street was completely carried away by the waves, and some of the windows of the Quebec Hotel were broken by the same means. The pavement in Bath Square was partially broken up, but no injury occurred to the Floating Bridge landing place.

These newspaper articles recorded the regularity of serious flooding events on Point and the damage that often occurred.

A typical flooding scene showing the west side of Broad Street in 1911. Image by S. Cribb.

As development expanded on Point, some areas were more susceptible to flooding than others, with Broad Street being particularly badly affected. This lead to residents installing slats in their entrances so that wooden floorboards could be dropped in, when necessary, and sealed up with Stamshaw clay, to prevent or minimise flooding.

Certainly, throughout much of the twentieth century, residents stoically accepted the situation, given that with the numerous slipways in the area and the low height of the sea defences it was inevitable that flooding would occur.

This picture taken in Bath Square during the 1950s shows a clearance underway after a storm had thrown shingle from Pickford's beach into the square.

A severe flood in Broad Street c. 1960.

Flooding in Broad Street 1984.

Although a number of improvements in the flood defences were made in the latter part of the twentieth century, there were two severe flooding events during this period: one in December 1989, and the other in January 1993 during which many houses were flooded in Broad Street.

10th January 1993.

The last significant flooding on Point – 10th January 1993. These four photos show the extensive area on Point that was affected by the flooding which occurred when a severe low pressure area combined with a very high spring tide and strong south westerly winds.

As new people moved into the area they were less accepting of this situation.
Eventually Portsmouth City Council obtained government finance to construct a £2 million comprehensive flood defence scheme for the area in 2005 which now protects residents from flooding.
This scheme included raising the defences in the harbour entrance, placing rock armour to break up the waves and dissipate their energy, and installing a number of flood gates that are closed at times of flood warnings.

East Street flood gates.

View from Round Tower looking north.

The "set back" wall and flood gates near
the *Still & West* pub.

The flood gates in Seager's Court.

A very high tide March 10th 2008 showing how well the flood defences performed.

Although this scheme has worked well to date, there is if course no guarantee that flooding can be prevented, since there is always a possibility that the combination of a very high spring tide, low pressure and a severe gale from the southerly quarter may result in overtopping of these defences in the future.

However, it is certainly hoped that the existing defences will perform well for many years to come, as they have been designed to incorporate sea level rise predictions in the future.
It should be realised that even with these new flood defences, the potential for flooding always exists due to floodwater rising naturally through the shingle spit; indeed during past flooding events this phenomenon could be seen, with water rising through drain covers and utility covers in the pavement and road. It is anticipated that with the recent improvements carried out to the drainage system in the area, this flood water would now be dealt with naturally.

For centuries it is apparent that residents of Point reluctantly accepted occasional flooding events as part of everyday life. It was only in the second half of the twentieth century that significant improvements were made to flood defences in the area and these resulted to a large extent because new residents in the area were not prepared to suffer this flooding and resultant damage.

Certainly in the 1950s there were still numerous undefended slipways on Point that regularly overtopped but today the current flood defences protect all the properties on Point, with the exception of the *Bridge Tavern* pub and the Land Rover BAR building.

Chapter 7

The East India Company

In the eighteenth century Portsmouth was growing in both size and importance. With this expansion came inevitable struggles relating to political dominance, which saw the emergence of considerable tension between the three most powerful men in the town: the yard commissioner, the garrison governor and the mayor.

Portsmouth was a major port of departure for expeditionary forces, and for both coastal and overseas trade, and was also regularly visited by crown heads, diplomats and senior service officers.
The town had connections worldwide and vessels from international trading people and companies were frequently at anchor at Spithead.

However, of all external influences, it was the East India Company that exerted most influence upon Portsmouth. [32]

The British East India Company was formed for the exploitation of trade with the East and South East Asia and India, incorporated by Royal Charter on 31st December 1600, and the first ships arrived in India at the port of Surat in 1608.

The company was formed to share in the East Indian spice trade which had been a monopoly of Spain and Portugal until the defeat of the Spanish Armada in 1588. It was met with opposition from the Dutch in the Dutch East Indies (now Indonesia) and the Portuguese, but the company's defeat of the Portuguese in India in 1612 won them trading concessions with the Mughal Empire.

During the next century the British gradually eclipsed the Portuguese who already held a political foothold in India. Their operations in India expanded and numerous trading posts were established along the east and west coasts of India.

The East India Company settled down to trade in cotton, silk goods, indigo and spices from south India and extended its activities to the Persian Gulf, South-East Asia and East Asia.

English communities developed around the large towns of Calcutta, Bombay and Madras and a royal dictat was issued from the Mughal Emperor, exempting the company from the payment of custom duties in Bengal.

At one point the company had the largest merchant navy in the world conducting and controlling a staggering 50% of the world trade.

After the mid-eighteenth century, tea became an important import to Britain from China. From the early nineteenth century, the company's tea trade with China was financed by illegal exports of opium to China which led to the Opium Wars, where the resulting defeat of China led to an increase and expansion of British trading privileges.

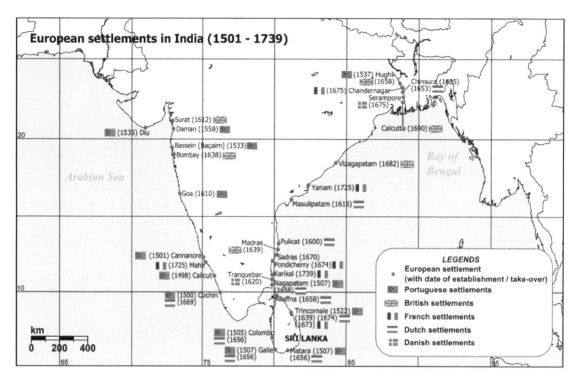

Map showing the distribution of settlements for the major European trading nations in India between 1501 and 1739.

When the company acquired control of Bengal in 1757, Indian policy was until 1773 influenced by shareholders meetings where votes could be bought by the purchase of shares. This led to government intervention and the Regulating Act of 1773 which established government control of political policy. The company's huge military expenditure nearly bankrupted the company, but the Regulating Act of 1773 placing India under the rule of a Governor General changed its fortunes.

Over the next forty years the company continued to expand until it eventually occupied the whole of India. Thereafter, they gradually lost both commercial and political control and its commercial monopoly was broken in 1813. From 1834 it was merely a managing agent for the British government of India.

However, in time, the annexation of native states, harsh revenue policies, and the plight of the Indian peasantry all contributed to the Rebellion of 1857-58, known as the Sepoy or Indian Mutiny.

After the Indian Mutiny its executive function was transferred to the Secretary of State for India and the India Office in 1858. It ceased to exist as a legal entity and was dissolved in 1874. [33]

Portsmouth had links with the company from 1608, but it was not until 1700 that they assumed solidarity and influence.

The increasing trade passing through Portsmouth resulted in expansion of the existing infrastructure with many new businesses opening up.
Carriers and innkeepers made money from the company and in addition food and drink were purchased locally, together with fresh provisions from local farmers.

The company developed an extensive organisation requiring the appointment of agents both home and abroad and in the southern half of the country there were thirteen agencies. Of these, Portsmouth was probably the most important port and is listed as being the oldest established agency, dating back to 1640.

Eight different men were employed as agents in the Portsmouth office throughout the eighteenth century and the work was very demanding, requiring both ability and scrupulous honesty. The agents were kept very busy delivering mail and packages and conducting their own correspondence with the company. Mail had to be collected, sorted and transferred to ships; weather forecasts had to be passed on to the Court of Directors; wages had to be checked; large sums of money handled, and the loading of silver supervised. [32]

The sailings were often numerous; indeed there were nineteen sailings from Portsmouth between March and June 1803, with destinations including China and multiple ports in India.

Sometimes, vessels were "lost" on voyages for numerous reasons including severe weather, hostilities or perhaps bad navigation. The advert below is for the auction of goods salvaged from the East India vessel, the *Henry Addington*, wrecked on the Bembridge Ledge, off the Isle of Wight. The *Star and Garter hotel* in Broad Street was widely used as an auction house.

CABLES, ANCHORS, GUNS, SHOT, PIG LEAD, &c. &c.

FOR SALE by AUCTION, at the STAR and GARTER TAVERN, Portfmouth, on FRIDAY the 3d of January, 1800, at Eleven o'Clock in the Forenoon,

101 Iron Guns of different Calibres from 1½ to 32 prs.

Anchors from 6 to 23 cwt. each.

22 Grapnels

20 Tons Shot different fizes.

1900 Pigs Lead.

3000 Bars Swedifh Iron.

174 Bolts Canvas.

Alfo a quantity of damaged Mufkets, Cutlaffes, Iron Knees, Bolt Iron, Copper, Dead Eyes, Blocks, and fundry other Ship's Stores, being faved from the Wreck of the Honourable Eaft India Company's fhip HENRY ADDINGTON, loft on Bembridge Ledge.

The fame may be viewed three days before the Sale, on application at the Office of Mr. ANDREW LINDEGREN, Portfmouth, where Catalogues may alfo be had.

Notice of auction held in the *Star and Garter* hotel for salvaged goods in 1800.

One of the most worrying activities for the agents was the supervision of silver loading operations. Substantial amounts were dispatched through the town for two very practical reasons: firstly to avoid marauding privateers from Ostend, St Malo, Dunkirk and Zealand, and secondly to avoid the corsairs of North Africa. As a result the fleet had a naval convoy as it approached its home waters.

The silver was needed in India for various company mints and the quantities moved through Portsmouth were significant: in February 1706 some £20,000 worth of bullion was sent from London by road for loading aboard two vessels. [32]

Portsmouth, with its reputation for violence, lawlessness and friction, was hardly the most suitable place and there were no banks before 1787, so the bullion was sometimes lodged in a private house.

The sense of responsibility and degree of activity involved could be substantial. Between 3rd April 1746 and 18 February 1747 George Huish, a Portsmouth agent for the company, supervised the loading of three hundred and sixty nine chests of silver aboard ten India bound vessels at Portsmouth. [32]

One of the most well-known Portsmouth agents was Andrew Lindegren, who was in office between 1788 and 1815 with his principal residence being sited at the northern end of Broad Street. He purchased what is now known as "The last house in Portsmouth" and its wharf in 1783, and the wharf became known as Lindegren's wharf.

Investment opportunities also presented themselves as the company was considered the safest and most profitable concern into which to sink money and an indeterminate number of Portsmouth businessmen invested.

Cargoes on board the vessels varied considerably between inward bound and outward bound. Outward-bound goods included carriages for officials in India, pictures, books, cutlery, saddles, scales, pewter ware, drums, buckets, glassware and firearms, together with lead, both sheet and bar. Inward-bound vessels from China included silver, tea and chests of skins and typical goods from India included raw silk, redwood and saltpetre.

Portsmouth became a much busier place at times of arrival of these ships and the navy was requested to provide escort ships in the Channel when their arrival was imminent, as the taking of the fleet would have been a tempting prize given that for example, an approaching fleet in August 1805 was said to be valued at £10 million. [32]

The company took all necessary measures to ensure that its monopoly was retained and any interlopers were dealt with firmly often by using its immensely powerful allies and connections, to prevent competition.

Smuggling from East India Company vessels was a constant problem for the Customs officers at Portsmouth and the act was often undertaken in a brazen way.

During the eighteenth century attempts were made to smuggle in goods including gold, tea, cloth and diamonds, and due to the potential problem, sometimes as many as eight Customs officers were placed aboard each vessel to ensure no smuggling took place.

Even with this degree of security it was reported that in May 1732 a passenger managed to come ashore at night carrying 126oz of gold. [32]

The smuggling of tea was also rife, although there were successes in finding contraband. The importation of goods from the East into the country made consumer goods more freely available to the public, and in the late eighteenth century there was an East Indian muslin warehouse sited in Broad Street.

View of Point, with sailing vessels in the Camber entrance as it would have been when the East India Company were trading. Painting by William Adolphus Knell (1801-1875) © Portsmouth Museum Service

During its existence, the company ran its own army, and men were often recruited from the local area, with Portsmouth serving as a port of embarkation. In the late eighteenth century the company actually retained a recruiting officer in Portsmouth and men were signed up for a period of five years.
These men were not all British and upstanding, as convicts were often recruited, together with men from other parts of the globe.

Sometimes the number of troops embarking was substantial as, for example, was recorded in this 1786 account:

> Two thousand troops belonging to the Prince of Hesse are embarked at Portsmouth to be sent to the East Indies in the service of the Company, to sail with the outward bound spring fleet.

In the mid to late eighteenth century several mutinies of these men occurred in Portsmouth and Spithead and on more than one occasion the mutineers ran amok in the town.

Other problems that occurred with their fleet on occasions when England was at war involved press gangs from the navy trying to impress the crew of East India vessels as they returned from the Far East.

In the eighteenth century the company was able to make use of the Royal Dockyard's repair facilities, but after taking advantage of the situation over several years they were forced to set up their own repair and maintenance facility in Portsmouth which may have been in the Camber, as their agent Lindegren had a storehouse and wharf there.

East India Company coat of arms.

East India Company currency.

In addition to the British East India Company, Portsmouth had regular visits from both the Dutch East India Company, a major competitor of the British East India Company that was superior in its number of vessels and trading links, and also the Swedish East India Company. During the first 20 years of the eighteenth century it is recorded that 50 outward bound vessels from the Dutch East India Company visited Portsmouth on their way to the East Indies.

It should be realised that the Dutch East India Company was a huge organisation similar to the British East India Company, and in fact had more vessels and trade than the British East India Company at one time.

The Dutch East India Company was established in 1602 and was granted a 21 year monopoly by the Dutch government to carry out colonial activities in Asia.
It was a more powerful company than the British East India Company, possessing quasi-governmental powers including the ability to wage war, imprison and execute convicts, negotiate treaties, coin money and establish colonies.

The company eclipsed all its rivals in Asia trade. Between 1602 and 1796 they sent almost 1 million Europeans to work in the Asia trade on 4785 ships, and netted more than 2.5 million tons of Asian trade goods.

By contrast, the rest of Europe combined sent only 882,412 people between 1500 and 1795 and the fleet of the British East India Company, the Dutch company's nearest competitor, was a distant second with its total traffic of 2690 ships and a mere one fifth of the tonnage of goods carried.

Weighed down by corruption, the Dutch East India Company went bankrupt and was formally dissolved in 1800.

The company's territories then became the Dutch East Indies and were expanded over the course of the nineteenth century to include the whole of the Indonesian archipelago (which in the twentieth century would form the Republic of Indonesia.)

The main European settlements in India during the period 1498 - 1739 were held by the Portuguese, English, French, Dutch and Danish.

The resultant effect on Portsmouth from all these East India Companies was positive as many additional jobs and much wealth was created from serving the needs of the ships and crew. In addition, people became more aware of the foreign lands in the East and their peoples, goods and customs. [34]

It is no exaggeration to state that the company changed the world. It created new communities, trading places and cities, and shaped countries and commercial routes. Singapore and Hong Kong were established by the company and India was shaped and influenced by it.

The East India Company had a major impact on eighteenth-century Portsmouth, creating jobs and investment possibilities and also bringing more people to the community who could tell of lands far away and the fabled wealth of the East. Some members of the local community were appointed as agents of the company. Building and ship repair work for the company brought more money to Portsmouth, together with the provisioning of vessels. Furthermore, the visits from the Dutch and Swedish East India Companies also boosted the local economy. [32]

All in all, the East India Company had an enormous impact on the world at large with its massive organisation of vessels, men and trade with the East, particularly during the eighteenth century. It also played a major role in influencing the history of Point.

Chapter 8

Watermen and Ferries Operating from Point

Due to its geographical position, Point has always been actively involved with transportation by water and as it developed over the years, so did the different forms of transport. Transportation by water for a fee has existed for centuries and the earliest means of travel by water from Point was either in wherries or hoys for local trips, or by larger vessels - initially by sail and later by steam, for longer journeys.

With the advent of steam, the popularity of wherries started to decline and steam ferries began operating from Point to Ryde on the Isle of Wight and a Floating bridge between Point and Gosport.
Finally, car ferries were developed in the nineteenth century to transport large goods such as horses and carriages, carts and cars between Point and Fishbourne on the Isle of Wight.

Gradually this trade from the Point by water came to an end for numerous reasons, one of which was its geographical position and physical constrictions for expansion.

Watermen

Watermen operating wherries and hoys were in existence for many years in Portsmouth harbour ferrying passengers locally on mainly short trips in the harbour and to the Isle of Wight, although they were occasionally known to make the trip across the English Channel to France. They were regularly used to take people and goods to and from the "Men of War" anchored at Spithead, and from ships anchored in the harbour.

Early records document sailing boats plying their trade in medieval times between Portsmouth and a place on the Isle of Wight near Ryde called Barnsley creek. However, when the creek silted up the traffic transferred to Ryde itself. [35]

By the 1600s boatmen were plying their trade from Ryde to Portsmouth, making a return crossing as frequently as every two hours.

The Lord of the Manor of Ashley and Ryde (Buckland) was responsible for these boats crossing Spithead, and the craft were known as Ryde or Portsmouth wherries. These boats were light rowboats used for transporting goods and passengers but sometimes the larger hoys were used.

Hoys were much larger vessels than wherries, usually about 60 tons and sometimes armed with small guns. Being of substantial size, some of these vessels plied their trade along the south coast, but the introduction of early steamers led to their gradual demise.

> The term "wherry built" means a boat without a wing transom, the ends of all the after planks terminating in the stern post, just as the bow planks do in the stem. The true wherry was an open boat has no gunwhale, and, if decked, no top rail to her bulwarks, the side timbers being all carried up through the water-ways, as high as, or in some cases a trifle above, the top strake. [36]

The first among the true wherries came from Portsmouth and Ryde and for all round good qualities, few open boats today excel these old sea cabs, which before the days of steam worked as ferries in all weathers between the mainland and the Isle of Wight. [36]

Portsmouth Wherry

The smaller class of these Portsmouth wherries used to ply their trade from Portsmouth Point and other places and were the same bumboats that tended the fleets in Nelson's time ferrying supplies, winter and summer, out among the punishing tides of Spithead.
The following passage outlines the procedure by which passengers were transferred into a wherry at Ryde for their journey:

> In times of favourable weather at high water the passengers were crammed promiscuously into a common luggage cart, till it was drawn out upon the almost level sands sufficiently far for a large wherry to float alongside, into which they were then transferred, and conveyed to the sailing packets, perhaps lying off at some considerable distance. [37]

This practice continued until Ryde had a substantial pier, built in 1814. This pier was extended on a number of occasions until in 1842 it saw the addition of a well-constructed pier-head that made it much easier for berthing alongside in order to embark or disembark passengers.

The ferrying of passengers outside Portsmouth Harbour, in particular, could be very dangerous in bad weather and numerous fatalities occurred over the years as watermen and their passengers were lost to the sea as the following newspaper articles confirm:

> A serious incident occurred in 1758 when 11 Jews were drowned as a sailing wherry capsized in windy weather when returning from anchored ships in Spithead with at least 20 Jews and others aboard, together with their effects.

One wonders whether the boat was somewhat overloaded.

> In 1761 a wherry coming from the Isle of Wight in which was Lieutenant Ferguson, of the Old Buffs, by which accident he was drowned; the wherryman was saved by some of the militia whom ventured their lives to save him.

The *Hampshire Telegraph* reported the following incident on December 22nd 1800:

> A wherry overset on Wednesday at Spithead with two watermen and a woman passenger in it; the two watermen were drowned, but the woman, although with great difficulty was fortunately saved.

In 1815 three Midshipmen from his Majesty's ship "Tiber" left their ship as a gale was commencing to come ashore to view a theatrical performance that evening. Unfortunately the wherry was pooped by a sea at the harbour entrance and was never seen afterwards. The waterman and a boy, together with the three Midshipmen all perished.

"*The Tour of Dr Syntax in search of the picturesque*" by Thomas Rowlandson.© Victoria and Albert Museum, London. This drawing shows how difficult it must have been in bad weather loading and unloading passengers from a wherry.

In October 1848, in a gale, two watermen took 5 women, visiting a fiancé, son and husbands to a vessel anchored at Spithead. Whilst tacking, the boat took on some water, and the frightened women rushed to one side of the boat causing it to capsize. They were in the sea for about 20 minutes before being rescued and one waterman and four women were drowned.

In addition to the vagaries of the weather, sometimes other serious incidents occurred. In 1813 the murder of a waterman was reported in the press:

A waterman named George Brothers was plied by three persons to take them to Ryde on the Isle of Wight to which he agreed and set sail for that purpose, but before they had started more than five minutes a scuffle was observed in the boat and the waterman thrown overboard. He was almost immediately picked up, covered with stabs and cuts and was quite dead. An alarm being given the wherry was followed by a boat from his Majesty's ship *Centaur*, and several other boats; these succeeded in coming up with and securing the three men, but not till after they had made a desperate resistance.

They were landed at Portsmouth amidst execrations of an almost ungovernable populace, and examined at the Town Hall; when they acknowledged themselves to be prisoners of war, and to have escaped from Forton prison at two o'clock in the afternoon.

It appears that they had been enabled by selling toys, to purchase entire new clothes by which they eluded the guards at the gate. Brothers left a wife and two children.

Some of these wherries were known to take occasional trips across the Channel after a small cargo of spirits etc. Around 1860 a small open wherry, named the *Johnny Broome*, was intercepted on a stormy morning some miles outside the Needles by a revenue cruiser, before her crew of two men had time to get rid of her little cargo of tubs. It was said that, owing to fatigue and the coarseness of the weather, those bold smugglers were not altogether sorry to be picked up, even by a revenue cutter. [36]

This story demonstrates how well designed and seaworthy these wherries were, and the ability of the crew to sail her across the English Channel in inclement weather at night confirms what excellent seamen they were.

Wherries had short masts, and when the mainsail was down and brailed in and then sailing under foresail and mizzen, she was under storm canvas and very handy when coming alongside an old fashioned battleship of the line, beneath all the projecting boats, booms davits etc. The wherry also rowed very well, and a well-built boat would last for years, being handed down from generation to generation.

Wherrymen used to ferry prostitutes to the Men of War anchored at Spithead, and the following account gives an idea of the procedure involved as a waterman selected suitable prostitutes:

> On the arrival of any man of war at Spithead, these girls (prostitutes) flock down to the shore, where boats are always ready, and here may be witnessed a scene somewhat similar to the trafficking of slaves in the West Indies. As they approached a boat, old Charon, with painter (rope) in hand, before they step aboard, surveys them from stem to stern, with the eyes of a bargaining Jew, and carefully culls out the best looking, and the most dashingly dressed; and, in making up his complement for a load, it often happens that he refuses to take some of them, observing (very politely) and usually with some vulgar oath; to one, that she is too old; to another, that she is too ugly; and that he shall not be able to sell them; and he'll be damned if he has any notion of having his trouble for nothing.

> The only apology that can be made for the savage conduct of these unfeeling brutes is, that they run a chance of nor being permitted to carry a cargo alongside, unless it makes a good shew-off; for it has often been known, that on approaching a ship, the officer in command has so far forgot himself as to order the waterman to push off – that he should not bring such a cargo of damned ugly devils on board, and that he would not allow any of his men to have them.

> At this ungentlemanly rebuff, the waterman lays up his oars a while, hangs his lip, musing on his mishap; and in his heart, no doubt cursing and doubly cursing the quarter deck fool, and

gradually pulls round to shore again, and the girls are not sparing of their abuse on the occasion.

Here the waterman is a loser, for he takes them conditionally; that is, if they are made choice of, or what he calls sold, he receives three shillings each; and, if not, then no pay; he has his labour for his pains; at least these were the terms at Portsmouth and Plymouth in war time at these great naval depots.

A boat usually carries about 10 of these poor creatures at a time, and will often bring off three cargoes of these ladies in a day; so that, if he is fortunate in his sales, as he calls them, he will make nearly five pounds by his three trips. [38]

From the start of development on Point which started in the late sixteenth/early seventeenth century, watermen have plied their trade, and it is documented that a regular ferry service between Portsmouth and Gosport was operational from sometime early in the sixteenth century. This proof is found in a document from the year 1602 at the end of the reign of Queen Elizabeth I which states that two Gosport men held the monopoly for this crossing and actually paid a rent to the Crown, and had been doing this for a number of years. [39]

This arrangement was cancelled by the Court and Commissioners were set up to ensure that the inhabitants of the borough of Gosport should provide 20 good and serviceable boats to always be ready and available to transport horsemen, footmen etc. and that one boat always be standing by on the Portsmouth side of the harbour.

A waterman served an apprenticeship of between 5 and 7 years, and boats were often handed down within families. Numbering was introduced at the beginning of the nineteenth century, with numbers painted on the hulls and sails, and the boats were regularly inspected for their seaworthiness.

Passengers at Point waiting to take a wherry in the mid nineteenth century.

The growth of the Dockyard provided much business for watermen over the years and during the Napoleonic wars in the early nineteenth century more than 1200 licenced wherrymen were stationed in the harbour, ferrying passengers, naval stores and equipment around the harbour and to the anchored ships.

These watermen were always ready to make money, often with sharp practices, and rates to take sailors back to their vessels after a run ashore were often outrageous, but with the urgency to get back aboard to avoid punishment for being late, they paid up.

Two sketches of *"Point watermen"* by Gabriel Bray in 1774. © National Maritime Museum, Greenwich, London.

One waterman's high prices was reported in *The Sporting Magazine*, Volume 27 in October 1805 by a visitor to Portsmouth:

> Portsmouth's watermen are more mercenary than their Publicans. I went to the Point to procure a boat to take me on board the *"Alexander"*, when one of the ferrymen hailed, I asked him how much he would expect to take me to the ship lying about a furlong from shore. It was a fair day and he demanded half a guinea. I offered him half a crown when the salt water savage bid me stay where I was, and be ******* , which must have been the case, if two naval gentlemen going off in their own boat had not witnessed the brutality, and kindly took me to the object of my desires.

Complaints were regularly received about the overcharging of some watermen, and finally in August 1812 the Gosport, Portsmouth and Portsea Ferry Act was introduced that dealt with the activities of watermen in Portsmouth harbour. Included within this Act was the mechanism to appoint a number of Commissioners to oversee the watermen.

The Act included regulations concerning fair and foul weather fares, hoisting of flags, setting of fares, location of flag hoisting signals, conditions relating to dangerous weather, trips taken outside the harbour, examinations and granting of licences, night fares, listing of approved watermen, special rules that applied to watermen that operated from outside of Portsmouth harbour, numbers of passengers allowed in boats, and a condition that regular meetings of the Commissioners were to be held alternately in Portsmouth and Gosport.

The following schedule lists some typical rates charged by wherrymen for trips in the harbour and for some trips outside the harbour. There was a very long schedule of rates document and this list is only a part of those in existence at that time.

WATERMEN'S FARES

Rates and Fares to be paid to Watermen limited and assessed by the Commissioners appointed under the Gosport, Portsmouth and Portsea Ferry Act, to commence on the first of May 1816.

FINE WEATHER FARES

To and From

GOSPORT, PORTSMOUTH AND PORTSEA

	s	d
Every passenger, not exceeding six, each	0	1
For the hire of a wherry, for one passenger, and not exceeding four	0	8
For five, and not exceeding six	1	0

FOUL WEATHER FARES

	s	d
Every passenger, and not exceeding six, each	0	3
For the hire of a wherry, for one passenger, and not exceeding four	1	0
For five, and not exceeding six	1	6

FINE WEATHER FARES

To be increased one half when the Blue Flag is hoisted and doubled in foul weather, when the red triangular flag is hoisted.

	s	d
For the hire of a wherry to Forton Mill	1	6
To Spithead, for one passenger, and not exceeding four	3	0
For returning with the same party	1	0
For five, and not exceeding eight	4	0
For returning with the same party	1	0
To more ships than one, each ship	0	6
For every passenger taken in at Spithead, not exceeding eight, each	0	6
To Cowes, for any number not exceeding eight	8	0
For returning with the same party	2	0

FREIGHT FOR CATTLE

	s	d
Horses, mules and bullocks in horse boats, each	2	0
Calves, sheep and hogs in wherries or other boats, each	0	3

FREIGHT FOR GOODS

	s	d
A wherry to St Helen's to take cases, bales, trunks etc. or other articles, not exceeding 8 cwt.	7	0

To Spithead, not exceeding 8 cwt	3	0
To the Motherbank, not exceeding 8 cwt	5	0
To Cowes, not exceeding 8 cwt	8	0
To Stokes Bay, not exceeding 8 cwt	4	0
To all vessels lying in the Harbour Channel, not exceeding 8 cwt	2	0

By 1823 an explanation of the flags hoisted was far more complex, with reference made to two flags hoisted one above the other, single white flags, red triangular flags and striped pendants alone or in combination. These signals related to rates inside and outside the harbour.

An 1823 list of rates written in a local Portsmouth Directory listed trips inside the harbour to numerous places including Forton Mill, Weovil Common, Wickor's Hard, Fareham, Portchester, Paulsgrove, Wymering and Portsbridge. There were also other destinations within the harbour.

Outside the harbour trips were included in the schedule to Southsea Castle, Haslar Barracks, Ryde, Nettlestone, Priory, Wootton, Hillhead, Brading, Stoke's Bay, Spithead, Motherbank, St Helen's Road, Middle Course and Cowes. In addition, further fare tariffs were included for cattle, goods and additions for working at night.

With the end of the Napoleonic Wars in 1815 came peace, and a fleet review, which provided huge trade for the watermen of the harbour.
However, after the wars there was a reorganisation in the Dockyard, resulting in the loss of jobs. The harbour became a quieter place, the French prisoners from the hulks had been repatriated and local criminals were housed there instead. In later years a good income was earned by watermen taking visitors to view the *Victory*, lying at anchor in the harbour. [39]

In 1821 an annual Point regatta was established and some of the events for watermen to compete in were very intensely contested.

The Point Regatta 1907 with large crowds and bunting strung across Broad Street. Photo taken by W.Stimson. © Portsmouth Museum Service.

However, the advent of steam powered ships marked the beginning of the demise of the centuries- old trade of ferrying people and goods around in a wooden boat propelled by oars or sail.

The first steam vessel visited the harbour in 1815 but it was the arrival of the first "Floating Bridge" in 1840, operating between the Point and Gosport, that really affected the trade of the watermen.

The watermen responded to this by later purchasing their own steam passenger ferries which they operated from Gosport to the Hard and this was later followed by the original Floating Bridge company operating their own steam launches for passengers which proved very successful.

The competition between the remaining watermen and the steam launches became intense and fights often broke out as landing places such as Point beach and the Hard became overcrowded.
Life became very hard for the watermen and their families, and in the late nineteenth century the poverty of many watermen forced them to sell or pawn their possessions and to rely on charitable food donations to feed their families. It was only those watermen that moved with the times that would survive the advent of steam in the long term.

In the early twentieth century, the wherrymen moored their boats at Point beach, and some of the owners were: J. Cottrell; W. Cottrell; J. Unwin; J. Butcher and Teddy Genge, and their boat names included *Cygnet, Why Not* and *Amelia.* There were also wherries moored at the Hard, Portsea, one of which was named the *Flying Cloud* which was the fastest and most famous of all the boats, with a crew of expert oarsmen who won many prizes at the annual Point regatta. Even the crew of the Royal Yacht *Victoria and Albert* could not beat the *Flying Cloud*, whose crew were J. Batchelor (steersman); J. Dukes; M. White; W. Grist and A. Cottrill.

The wherry course in the regatta was from the Point, across the harbour, then around the *Victory* - at that time moored in the harbour just off Gosport - then back across the harbour to pass the finishing line near the committee boat, the *Duchess of Kent*, which was a paddle boat of the Isle of Wight Ferry company.
There were rowing races for all at the regatta, including girls, and there was a "coal shovellers" race which involved four men to each boat, each man using a pointed coal shovel instead of oars. There were also tub races for men who sculled the tubs along with short oars, and the greasy pole and pillow fight competition. Unsurprisingly, these regattas proved very popular. In 1919, the famous wherry, *Flying Cloud* was at last beaten in a challenge match by a wherry built for the occasion by Mr George Feltham, a well-known local boat builder of Broad Street, Point. (A detailed account of this race and lead up is contained in Chapter 14 of this book.)

Transportation by sail and steam.

As Point became developed, businesses were soon set up to provide travel by water to numerous places locally and also to foreign ports. Adverts were placed in newspapers, and many of the local pubs on Point acted as points of contact where more information and bookings could be made.
These pubs included the *Navy Tavern*, *Thatched House*, *Star & Garter*, *Roebuck* and the *Still & West* among others. The vessels undertaking these voyages were of various sizes, with the larger vessels capable of crossing oceans.

Boats were available to take people to many local places including Gosport, Fareham and other places within the harbour, the Isle of Wight, Lymington, Poole, Plymouth and Havre in France. There were also passages available to destinations as far away as India.

Initially voyages were carried out under sail but in the nineteenth century, after the development of the steamship, fewer voyages were undertaken by sail.

Portsmouth was fast becoming Britain's premier naval port, and by 1796 the first twice daily regular sailing packet called the *"Packet"* operated between Ryde and Portsmouth from *the Bugle Inn* to the *Quebec Hotel* on Point.

CAPITAL CONVEYANCE between Portf-mouth & Ryde, by a regular Poft-office Packet, carrying the mail, which will fail every morning at 9 o'clock, from the Weft India and Quebec Tavern, Bath-fquare, Portfmouth, for RYDE; and return every afternoon at half paft three, from the Bugle Inn, Lower Ryde, for PORTSMOUTH, in time to fave any of the London Coaches. There will alfo be a COACH, at Ryde, on the arrival of the Mail, to take Paffengers to Newport. The Mafter to be fpoken with at the Weft India and Quebec Tavern, Portfmouth; and at the Bugle Inn, and Hotel, Ryde. A commodious decked Veffel for the purpofe.

In 1817 the following list of destinations was printed in the Addenda of *"The History of Portsmouth"* written by Lake Allen:

A Packet sails to Ryde every morning at 9 o'clock, and afternoon at 3 o'clock from the *Quebec Tavern*, Point;
A Packet to Cowes every afternoon at half past two o'clock from the *Kings Head*, Point;
A Packet to Lymington, three times a week from the *Thatched House*, Point;
The Southampton Hoy sails from the *White Hart*, Point, on Tuesdays, Thursdays and Saturdays – the time of sailing depends on the tide;
To Plymouth and Torbay, three times a week from the *Neptune & Mars*, Point;
To Poole, Horaman's vessel sails from the *King's Head*, Point every Friday, and Manlaw's vessel on every Tuesday, Thursday and Saturday from the *Roebuck*, Point;
To Guernsey, once a week from the *True Blue,* on the Point;
Boats go every day to Portchester, but the time depends on the tide.

In the *New Portsmouth Guide of 1835* other destinations are included:-

Steam Packets

To Cork, Dublin and Liverpool calls in at Portsmouth (*Blue Posts*) on the route;
To New York from London via Portsmouth on certain dates – agent Garratt and Gibbon, Bath Square;
To Havre from Southampton via Portsmouth – Wheeler's office, Broad Street.

Packet – Wherries

Bembridge twice daily from the *Three horseshoes*, Bath Square;
In addition to the above destinations, the *Quebec Tavern* dealt with passengers that wanted a passage to India and the Far East and had regular sailings to Havre-de-Grace in France.

Later in the mid-19th century the *Star and Garter* in Broad Street also advertised Steam Packets to Ryde, Cowes, Southampton, Plymouth, Havre and America.

In 1817, prior to the introduction of steam, a Packet would have been a sailing Packet, defined as a vessel employed to provide a regular scheduled service carrying freight and passengers. By 1834 steam Packets left the *Quebec Tavern* for Ryde four times daily during the winter months, five times daily during May and half way through June, and eight times daily during the summer.

It indicates what a vibrant place Point must have been at that time with so many Packets coming and going to various ports locally, along the coast and to foreign nations. It is also somewhat surprising that there were such a large number of establishments, usually pubs, which dealt with this trade.

The sailing Packets at the beginning of the nineteenth century in 1802 on the passage to Havre from the *Quebec Tavern* were 40 and 90 tons respectively, and the voyage to Plymouth in 1803 would have been on a 25 ton smack called the *"Daniel"*.

In 1817 the first steam vessel to operate between Portsmouth and Ryde went into service. However, the 15hp, 70 ton *"Britannia"* which was originally designed for the crossing between London and Southend, was withdrawn after 4 weeks of her maiden voyage across the Solent due to not being of a suitable design to cope with the adverse winds and strong tides. [40]

On April 5th 1825, The Union Steam Packet, run by the Portsmouth & Ryde United Steam Packet Company, first started between Ryde and Portsmouth carrying passengers, wheeled vehicles and livestock. To celebrate the day, two hogsheads of beer were given to the watermen and others at Ryde Pier, and a like quantity at the *Quebec Hotel*, Portsmouth. [13]

An early steam passenger vessel approaching the *Quebec Hotel*.

This service prospered with a succession of paddle steamers, *Arrow* (1825), *Lord Yarborough* (1826), and *Earl Spencer* (1833), and by 1842 up to ten daily sailings were being made from Ryde to Portsmouth's new Victoria Pier at the Sally Port, which opened in 1842.

This old painting c. 1828 shows passengers disembarking from a ferry berthed to the north of and adjacent to the *Quebec Hotel.* (the building on the right hand side is the *Isle of Wight tavern.*)

In 1846 the Albert Pier was constructed at Portsea, stretching some 1200ft into Portsmouth harbour, allowing the steamers to embark and disembark passengers, and by 1847 the first railway link to London from Portsmouth via Brighton was opened. Passengers were then moved by omnibus between Portsmouth Station and Victoria Pier for their onward voyage to the Isle of Wight.

With competition intensifying, and the opening of Clarence Pier to the public in 1861, many steamers on the Portsmouth to Ryde trip called in here and passenger traffic to Victoria Pier began to decline.

W. Fisher & Co, 66 Broad Street, circa 1910. They were general carriers and the advert on the wall refers to steamers calling in at Southampton, Plymouth and Falmouth.

Gosport ferries between Point and Gosport

Prior to 1840, transportation to and from Portsmouth Point and Gosport across the harbour for passengers, and some goods, was primarily by wherries; those travelling with horses, carriages or carts faced a 14 mile journey by road.

Although a horse ferry was introduced in 1834, a group of local businessmen thought that the idea of a "Floating Bridge" was a worthwhile project worth pursuing. Initially, two routes were proposed, both from the same location in Gosport: - one to serve the Point, and the other to the old Gunwharf, serving Portsea.

Following objections from the Admiralty to the proposals for two bridges, a single bridge was finally decided upon, and the route chosen was between Gosport and Point.

An Act of Parliament had to be obtained, and this was done even though Parliament had been petitioned by 1100 watermen urging the rejection of the proposal. Unfortunately for the watermen they had little support from the general public who supported the proposal.

Since there was insufficient room available on the beach at Point to accommodate both the new Floating Bridge and the existing watermen, additional land had to be acquired. To resolve this problem, part of Mr Lindegren's private premises were purchased and demolished, to allow an extension of the slipway. [41]

The first "Floating Bridge" was built in 1840 by F. W. Acraman in Bristol and was designed by James Meadows Rendel. [42]
This first vessel, named 'Victoria' was guided by chains and was soon joined by a sister ship, 'Albert', manufactured by the same company in 1842.

After being towed around the coast from Bristol, the "Victoria" set off on her maiden voyage across Portsmouth harbour on May 4th 1840 and made the crossing in 12 minutes amid much fanfare by thousands of interested onlookers. This was somewhat later than originally scheduled as can be seen from the following newspaper article:

> The Floating Bridge across Portsmouth Harbour has been several days experimentally at work and today performed its trips on the average of six minutes and a half. It will commence its public transits on the 11th March and will continue daily from 7am until 9pm until the month of May; leaving Gosport at the hours and half hours and Portsmouth at the intermediate quarters, excepting on the Sabbath when the bridge will not work during the hours of Divine service [43]

A lithograph showing an early floating bridge crossing the harbour. © of the British Library Board.

The first vessel was 100 feet in length and 60 feet wide with two steam engines driving heavy oak cogs that engaged on the heavy chains laid out across the harbour. It was capable of transporting carriages, carts, horses and even cattle as well as foot passengers.

The original fare was 1 penny for passengers. There were charges laid out for horses with coaches, chariots etc. and also for sheep, cattle, bath chairs, wheelbarrows, heavy waggons etc.

During the first 6 months the bridge catered for 220,000 passengers, 13,965 carriages, 3,964 horses and 1,763 cattle, as well as carrying the mail coach for London and other vehicles on their way from Portsmouth to link up with the L.S.W.R. station at Southampton. [39]

In 1864 the *"Victoria"*, now worn out, was replaced by a new vessel, the *"Alexandra,* "and in 1891 the *"Albert"* sunk and was replaced by the *"Duchess of York"*.

Floating bridge *"Alexandra"*

These two "Floating bridges" were in service for many years, before being withdrawn due to the poor condition of both in December 1959. The area of Old Portsmouth and the Point was also waning in importance compared to other areas of Portsmouth. In addition, the fact that the Government abolished petrol rationing in 1952 caused a loss of business, as many companies drove their vehicles from Portsmouth to Gosport and back as it was a cheaper option.

Prior to the closure of these bridges, the queues of traffic in Broad Street were often very long, stretching down the road, often parallel to a queue of traffic on the other side of the road waiting to board the Isle of Wight car ferry.

Isle of Wight car ferries.

With the increasing development of Portsmouth and the Isle of Wight in the nineteenth and twentieth centuries, businesses sought a better means of transporting their goods across the Solent, and the era of the motor car was also fast approaching.

Until 1925 there were towboat operations in place, transporting a limited number of vehicles, goods and livestock between Portsmouth Point and Ryde Esplanade, and in 1925, the last year of operation transported 1718 cars. These towboat operations were started c.1825.

One captain of these large 60 feet tow boats often used to take some of the local boys from the Point that could swim, on a trip to the island. The children used to swim from the tow boat that lay offshore, owing to the receding tide, after the cargo had been dispatched. On the return journey "Skipper Lewis" used to then give the boys a glorious meal of bread and pigs' trotters, purchased at Ryde, after the boat had been washed down.

This tow boat operation was then transferred to Fishbourne in 1926 with improved facilities and in that year the total number of cars carried reached nearly 4000. [44]

This famous photo of a towboat used to transport livestock was given to me many years ago by the young lad fifth from the right holding a stick, Sam Loader, a well-known character who lived in the old *Fortitude Tavern* building in Broad Street for many years and was regularly seen having a swim off the Point in his later years.

This mode of transportation was revolutionised in 1927 with Southern Railway introducing the first car ferry operating on this route, the "*M. V. Fishbourne*". She was 131 feet in length and carried 18 cars with a crossing time of 55 minutes from the slipway at Broad Street on Point to the Fishbourne slipway.

She started operating two return crossings daily on the route, and in the following year a slightly larger sister ship, the "*M. V. Wootton*", was introduced to what was already becoming a very popular route. In 1930 another ferry, the "*M. V. Hilsea*", was added.

During the Second World War the original two ferries were commandeered for military service as minesweepers, and sailed to Dunkirk, but were not used in the evacuation exercise. After the war, all three vessels continued on the route for some time until they were unable to cope with the increasing demand, and improvements were needed to the shore based facilities.

Therefore in 1960, new facilities costing £1million were built in the Camber, adjacent to East Street, when a purpose built slipway, car parking and booking office facilities were constructed.

Works underway on the construction of the new East Street slipway and terminal in 1960.

A car ferry berthed at the then new East Street slipway.

At Fishbourne a new wider slipway was built, together with a large marshalling area. This work was overseen and paid for by the British Transport Commission who now operated the ferries on this route. In addition, two new purpose-built ferries were constructed, the "*M. V .Camber Queen*" and the "*M. V. Fishbourne*", doubling the capacity of the route, as these ferries could each carry 34 cars and 165 passengers. [44] The crossing time was also reduced to 45 minutes and an hourly service maintained with foot passengers allowed for the first time.

In 1963 a total of 54,919 cars were transported on the route. Due to increasing demand another larger ferry, the *"M.V.Cuthred"*, was introduced to the route in 1969 which was capable of carrying 48 cars and 400 passengers.

In 1973 British Rail named their shipping division Sealink and with the need for ever increasing capacity a fourth car ferry was added to the route in the form of the even larger *"M. V. Caedmon"*, which could carry 52 cars and 756 passengers with an increased service speed of 11 knots.

Unsurprisingly, the Broad Street terminal had been outstripped by the number of vehicles wishing to travel to the Isle of Wight, and bookings had to be made months in advance. A new much larger terminal and car park was therefore constructed on the other side of the Camber Dock adjacent to Gunwharf Road on the site of the old dry dock and was opened in 1982.

The old Camber dry dock before conversion to the IOW car ferry terminal.

In 1983 a larger ferry still, the *"M. V. St Catherine"*, was added to the ever growing fleet, being 77 metres in length carrying 142 cars and 1000 passengers and capable of making the crossing in 35 minutes. Later in the same year her sister ship, the *"M. V. St Helen"* entered service.

In 1987 a third ferry was added to the fleet, the *"M. V. St Cecilia,"* being joined in 1990 by another, the *"M. V. St Faith"*, both built in England for the company, now called Wightlink.

Further increased capacity was needed in 2001 and the vessel the "*M. V. St Clare*" was introduced to the fleet, having been constructed in Poland. She was 86 metres in length and capable of carrying over 180 cars and 770 passengers and she is a double ended design like the original ferries on the route.

St Clare leaving Portsmouth harbour. She operates at 13.5 knots and has the most superior facilities of any ship operating to the Island. With 5 ferries, Wightlink are now able to meet the demand from locals and visitors to the Isle of Wight, so important to the island's economy.

The progression and expansion of the car ferry service in the relatively short period of 87 years is quite remarkable and the huge number of passengers and cars transported to and from the Isle of Wight today bears a striking contrast to the towboats of the early twentieth century. With the service still operating flat out in the peak summer months, one wonders when the next expansion of ferries and infrastructure will have to occur to accommodate the demand for a service that people take for granted today.

Trips around the harbour.

It was only those watermen that moved with the times that survived the advent of steam in the long term. Firms such as J. Butcher & Sons Ltd, established in 1809 as licenced Watermen and Foy boatmen, were one such business that did so and were in existence until 2013, hiring out their boats and services for more than 200 years, and their blue boats were a common sight around the harbour, particularly in the Camber.

J.Butcher & Son's fleet of boats moored in the Inner Camber.

They had their offices in the Camber together with moorings, a slipway and workshop facilities. They were either assisting shipping entering or leaving the harbour, or in the summer months utilising some of their fleet of boats to ferry tourists around Portsmouth Harbour to see all the warships in port. They were a well-known fleet to locals and their boats were always very smart and well maintained.

Successors to the original watermen continued to offer trips around the harbour for many years, some still operating from Portsmouth Point.

The *Portsmouth Belle* used to be operated by Maurie Pearce setting off from Portsmouth Point and the Hard for many years carrying passengers on sightseeing trips around Portsmouth harbour. She was originally named the *Folkestone Belle,* built at Cowes, Isle of Wight in 1928, and was one of the Little Ships of Dunkirk that rescued British troops from the beaches in 1940. She transported 100 men back from the beaches along with many other small craft from England having been temporarily requisitioned from her job as the Hayling ferry in 1940 to help with the evacuation.

The *Portsmouth Belle (ex.Folkestone Belle).*

This brass plaque from the Portsmouth Belle was awarded to vessels that are members of the Association of Dunkirk Little Ships that took part in the evacuation of troops from Dunkirk in 1940.

In the mid-1980s the watermen began to operate a circular waterbus service around the attractions of Portsmouth harbour. The boats remained owned by individuals but proceeds were shared. All boats received a pale blue livery. The Portsmouth Harbour Ferry Company (PHFC) initially joined this consortium using two blue boats of their own, but withdrew in 1996. These trips around the harbour are still very popular in the summer months, but today none of the vessels currently operate from the Point or Camber.

Chapter 9

Coach and Bus Transportation

As Point developed throughout the seventeenth and eighteenth centuries, the need for suitable overland transport to reach Portsmouth from London and other parts of the country became essential and coaching inns and hotels established themselves at the Point and in the nearby streets, particularly the High Street.

One of the earliest references of overland travel to Portsmouth is written in Charles. G. Harper's *"The Portsmouth Road and its Tributaries: Today and in Days of Old."* In it he refers to three sixteenth-century Inspectors of Ordnance:

> July 20th 1532, Xpofer (Christopher) Morays, gunner, Cornelys Johnson, the Maister Smythe and Henry Johnson being reimbursed for their costs in riding to Portismuthe to view the King's Ordnance there.

The following phrase from a public announcement towards the end of the seventeenth century seems to hint at the dangers and problems relating to coach travel at that time :

> Ye Portsmouth Machine sets out from Ye "Elephant and Castell" and arrives presently by the Grace of God. [5]

The Navy Records Society published an interesting description of a journey to Portsmouth written by an employee of the Navy Pay Office in January 1728-29:

> We had a frozen journey from London in three days travelling with money on the coach. Our guard was eight horse Grenadier Guards, with a subaltern officer.
> It snowed a great part of the way, and I think they had a bad time of it, for we could hardly keep ourselves warm with glasses up; yet the officer would not let the troopers put on their cloaks, to inure them (I suppose) to bad weather and discipline. Two of them ride before the coach and the rest followed.
> We stopped at inns for the night and all ate well and the money was kept in the guard room with the soldiers. [5]

The Navy Post Office was located at Point and the article indicates how slow the coach journey between London and Portsmouth was at that time.

Before metalled roads were established during the sixteenth and seventeenth centuries, road repairs were the responsibility of Parish councils and as they were not paid for this work, the procedure was highly ineffective. The roads were often potholed, narrow, rutted and sometimes impassable, muddy in winter and indistinguishable from the surrounding countryside in places and were the resort of highway men.

In the mid sixteenth century this would not have caused too many problems as there was very little wheeled traffic and what there was would have been local traffic, so failures would not have been too troublesome. By the 17th century it was clear local taxes were needed to supplement this statute labour, but even a combination of statute labour and taxes was still insufficient for this purpose.

During the seventeenth century the amount of wheeled traffic grew between London and Portsmouth which was rapidly expanding.

Because the roads were not being adequately maintained for this new traffic growth, the road was becoming partially ruinous, in part due to the regular loads of her Majesty's stores. A petition was presented to the Government for a solution, since the section of road between Petersfield and Butser was almost impassable for 9 months of the year.

Parliament agreed, and in 1711 the Portsmouth and Sheet Turnpike Act was passed. The entire road between Petersfield and Portsmouth was covered by the act, and tolls could be collected to pay for the maintenance of the road. The control of these turnpikes was placed in the hands of selected trustees who were men of local importance.

Different rates were charged for animals and coaches, and some types of traffic were exempt from charges, such as mail horses and coaches, funeral goers, churchgoers, soldiers and their baggage carts.

The advent of turnpikes also led to the faster delivery of mail. Although a public postal service existed from the first part of the seventeenth century, the post was carried by post boys on horses and the process was slow and very dangerous with robberies being commonplace. This system continued for about 150 years until by 1785 mail coach routes were introduced in the UK to important destinations including Portsmouth.

Before this time when only slow stages were running, a journey from London to Portsmouth took 14 hours in good weather.

These new mail coaches in 1785 were provided by contractors and maintenance was big business as the coaches had to be regularly cleaned and oiled and an income could be had undertaking this maintenance work, in addition to collecting passengers fares.

The average speed of these early coaches was usually 7-8 mph in summer and about 5mph in winter but the speed increased as the road quality improved.

The Post Office sent a guard with all mail coaches who was heavily armed with two pistols and a blunderbuss. The official uniform of the guards included a black hat with a gold band and a scarlet coat with blue lapels and gold braid.

The upper part of the coach was painted black, while the door and lower panels were maroon, and the wheels were painted in Post Office red. The initial coaches had four passengers inside with a driver, which was increased to three outside with the introduction of a double seat behind the driver.

The coach travelled faster than a stage coach and stopped only where necessary for postal business and the contractors organised fresh horses to be available at stages on the route.

Thomas Rowlandson print (c.1790s) entitled *"The Portsmouth Fly"* showing the stagecoach racing down the hill towards Portsmouth. © Portsmouth Museum Service.

With the establishment of these coach services, coaching inns grew up around the country and on Point the principal coaching inns included the *Blue Posts* and the *Star and Garter* in Broad Street, and the *Quebec Hotel* in Bath Square. The *Van Office* was located opposite on the corner of Bathing Lane providing trade in travel by vans similar to stage coaches but much larger.

Other pubs were advertised as pick up points for passengers and parcels, including the *Navy Tavern* and the *Kings Arms* in Broad Street and the *Still Tavern* and the *Isle of Wight Tavern* in Bath Square.

> The famous "*Flying machine*" of Messrs Clark' regularly travelled between London and Portsmouth. This coach offered an experience which was so little like flying that it took an entire day to complete the journey, leaving the *King's Arms* in Portsmouth every Monday, Wednesday and Friday at 10pm and returning on alternate nights, together with another machine which arrived and set off from the *Blue Posts*. [45]

Other Clark's waggons set off from the *White Hart* in Broad Street in the 1780s.

In "*Cary's New Itinerary, Hampshire 1815*" numerous coach routes between London and Portsmouth were listed. The schedule included many starting points in London such as the *Bolt-In-Tun,* Fleet Street, the *Bull and Mouth*, Bull and Mouth Street, the *Golden Cross*, Charing Cross and the *Spread Eagle*, Gracechurch Street. The main destinations of these coaches on Point were the *Blue Posts* and also the *Quebec Tavern*, where connections could be made with the Isle of Wight Packets for passengers and parcels going to Ryde.

Thomas Rowlandson print entitled *"Miseries of travelling"* c. 1807 showing how chaotic and crowded coach travel could be at that time. (c) National Maritime Museum, Greenwich, London.

The following adverts inserted in the *Hampshire Telegraph* between 1800 and 1818 give a good indication of the different establishments where coaches picked up passengers and goods.

ROCKET—RESPECTABLE LIGHT COACH.

JOHN CROSS and Co. return their most grateful thanks to their numerous Friends in Portsmouth, Portsea, Gosport, and the Isle of Wight, for the very liberal support their coach has experienced, and humbly solicit a continuance of their favours; and beg to inform them, that, for their further accommodation, the ROCKET COACH will now travel EVERY DAY, Sundays included, at 9 o'clock in the Morning, from the Fountain Inn, High-street, and Quebec Tavern, Bath-square, Portsmouth, and at the George and Red Lion, Queen-street, Portsea, to the White Bear, Piccadilly, and Belle Sauvage, Ludgate-Hill, London :—Performed in 9 Hours, by JOHN CROSS, EDWARD WHITE, and HENRY LEVETT.

N.B.—Families accommodated by being taken up and put down at their own Residences.

ORIGINAL LONDON POST COACH.

WILLIAM CLARK and ROBERT CLINCH, BEG leave to inform their Friends and the Public, this Coach fets out every evening at Six o'Clock, from the Two Blue Pofts Inn, and Still Tavern, on the Point, and from their Office, No. 61, Queen-ftreet, Town of Portfea; to the Spread Eagle and Crofs Keys Inns, Gracechurch-ftreet, and Golden Crofs, Charing Crofs, London; and returns from thence every evening at the fame hour. CLARK and Co. pledge themfelves that no exertions, on their part, fhall be wanting to render their Coaches equal to any on the road, and which they truft will infure them that countenance and fupport they have hitherto enjoyed the preference of. Likewife, from the above Tavern, the London Day Coach, to the Golden Crofs, every morning at Five o,Clock; and a Light Night Coach, carrying only four infides, every evening at Seven o'Clock. WM. CLARKE's original London Waggons, as ufual, every morning at Eleven o'Clock, to the White Hart and King's-Head Inns, Borough; and, for the better accommation of his friends, wifhing their goods from the City, he has opened the White Horfe, Friday-ftreet, Cheapfide, from whence goods are punctually forwarded.

☞ Flying Waggons on the fhorteft Notice.

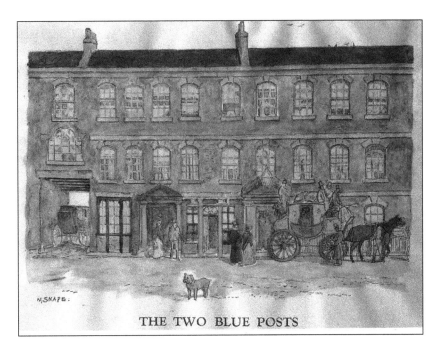

THE TWO BLUE POSTS

The famous coaching house located in Broad Street - *The Two Blue Posts*.
(Based on the sketch in the Illustrated History of Portsmouth by William. G. Gates)

```
WITH A GUARD
LONDON, PORTSMOUTH, and PORTSEA
COACHES, to the BOLT-IN-TUN INN,
FLEET-STREET, LONDON:
SET out every Evening, at Six o'Clock,
  from the FOUNTAIN INN, HIGH-STREET,
PORTSMOUTH, and arrive there every Morning early.
Alfo fet out from the BOLT-IN-TUN INN, FLEET-
STREET, LONDON, for PORTSMOUTH and PORTSEA,
every Evening at the fame hour. Call going and
coming at the BELL INN, GRACECHURCH-STREET,
and OLD SHIP INN, BOROUGH, LONDON. Paffen-
gers and Parcels taken up at the STAR and GARTER
and NAVY TAVERNS, on the Point, and at the
GEORGE TAVERN, QUEEN-STREET, PORTSEA.
    ☞ Office and Warehoufe, No. 63, BROAD-
STREET, on the POINT.
    Performed by { GEORGE FIELDING,
                  { JAMES WHITE and Co.
   *₊* Parcels above 5l. value muft be entered as
fuch, and paid for accordingly.
         ☞ Security for any Truft.
   The old original LONDON WAGGONS, every
Day to the OLD SHIP INN, Borough, and CROSS
KEYS, WOOD-STREET, CHEAPSIDE.—Extra Wag-
gons on the fhorteft notice.
```

Throughout the period between 1775 and 1840 a number of famous names of coaches appear in the advertisements, such as the *Hero, Tantivy, Nelson, Times, Rocket, Regulator, Dart, Independent* and *Royal Mail*.

The distances to destinations in London from Portsmouth were measured from the seaward end of Broad Street and during the latter part of the eighteenth century the trip to and from London took 14 hours.
However, in the 1820s the *Rocket* was the speediest coach on the road taking 9 ½ hours from Charing Cross to the *Blue Posts* and night coaches at that time took approximately 12 hours.

As well as the many coaches leaving and arriving at Point, there were also numerous waggons and vans (carriers), and in Holden's Portsmouth Directory of 1811, 5 separate companies are Listed:

Hoare and Stanbury's Fly waggons from the *Blue Posts Hotel*.
Pescott's waggons and vans from 46 Broad Street to London.
Cox's vans from 57 Broad Street to London.
Matthew's waggons from the *Blue Posts* to Brighton.
Garnett's waggons from the *Blue Posts* to Fareham.

The Van office

The Van Office was never as famous as the other well-known coaching houses such as the *Quebec*, and the *Blue Posts* on the Point, as the vans were mainly used to carry merchandise.

The office also served as a booking office for some well-known line of coaches. They were much slower than stage coaches, with the trip to London taking from 15 to 16 hours in good weather, but in unfavourable weather it would take much longer.

These vans were mainly used for goods traffic but a few passengers were carried, although not in comfort. In 1805 the customers were mainly bluejackets (sailors) and the cost to travel on the outside of a van was 6s. 6d, whereas for a swifter more comfortable coach the cost was £1. 1s. 0d for an inside berth and 12s. 6d outside. [46]

One of the vans left the Portsmouth office at 4pm every day for the *Eagle*, City Road, London, arriving there at about 7am or 8am the next morning and another van left London at this time bound for Portsmouth.

The Van Office, Bath Square.
(demolished in 1894)

.

The Van Office - part of a photo dated 1861. The building is the one in the centre of the photo in Bath Square on the corner of Bathing Lane.

By the mid-1830s coaches on the Portsmouth road were running on borrowed time as the railways were steadily reaching out and it was inevitable that Portsmouth would eventually be linked with the capital. Trains were operational by 1840 and although coaches ran for several years after this they had no hope of competing with the 3 hour schedule of the railways.

The coach driver Andrew Nance of Portsmouth, whose father had owned the *Blue Posts* in Broad Street and the *Fountain Hotel* and *Crown* in the High Street made the journey by coach from Portsmouth to London in the fastest recorded time in 1839. In his obituary published in the *Hampshire Telegraph*, it stated that he was generally regarded as the best four in hand driver in the country. In recording his record time in the *Tantivy* he covered the distance in 5 hours and 42 minutes pipping his rival, Dick Faulkner, driving the *Dart* by 6 minutes.

However, it was widely accepted that the difference between the usual coaching time of 8 ½ hours and 5 hours 42 minutes was too great to be accomplished by the skill of the driver. Sam Carter, an experienced coach driver who worked for Andrew Nance tells how:

> I used to drive the *Tantivy*, a day and night coach, which afterwards ran only by day. We drove from Portsmouth to Farnborough station, then put the coach on the train, and drove into town from the terminus at *Nine Elms*.

1841 was the year that the Portsmouth Mail coaches ceased running and transferred to the railways. Prior to this a dozen mail coaches ran from Portsmouth to London, Oxford, Bristol and other places. The first railway in Portsmouth opened in June 1847.

Coaching tales

Coach travel between Portsmouth and London was an uncomfortable and sometimes dangerous experience and highwaymen were often encountered on the route.

The articles below published at the time in the *Hampshire Telegraph* in the eighteenth and nineteenth centuries and in other newspapers describe events and accidents of that time:

The first account describes an occasion when a baby boy was born whilst on the journey.

> On Wednesday last, about an hour after the Portsmouth Stage set out, a poor woman in the basket was delivered of a male child: They would have had the woman got out, but she would not be prevailed on; on which account the humanity of the coachman to London cannot be too much commended, as he would not admit any men into the basket, but only two women, one of whom was her companion, and on her account drove gently thro' every town they came to that was paved. The Company in the Coach subscribed to her relief. (1766)

The next three accounts describe incidents when coaches overturned injuring passengers, sometimes due to equipment failure, but in one of these instances due to the coach driver being under the influence of alcohol.

> On Monday last at five o'clock, in the morning, the coach from Portsmouth, on its way to London, with six inside, and seven or eight outside passengers, was overset near the Devil's Punch Bowl, seven miles from Godalming, and the passengers much hurt; a woman, one of the inside passengers, far gone with child, had her body and leg much bruised, and was left at Godalming in a very dangerous state; some money was subscribed by the passengers for her relief; another woman, inside, had some of her teeth knocked out, and was much disfigured. This accident was imputed to the neglect of the coachman and postilion, who had stopped several times to drink, and when the coach was overset, it was out of the road on a bank, where it had run for some minutes by the track of the wheels.(1770)

> On the night of Sunday the 9th, between 11 and 12 o'clock, as the Portsmouth mail was proceeding from Guildford to Ripley, the leader's reins broke, in consequence the coachman lost his command of them; and owing to a strange horse being put to at the last change, the coach was run against a bank and upset, whereby the coach was nearly broken to pieces, and the coachman was thrown from his box and most dreadfully mangled; his cheek bone being shattered, his shoulder dislocated, and otherwise seriously hurt. The guard and other passengers escaped with very little injury. (July 1815)

> Tuesday evening, one of the Portsmouth coaches was upset near Cobham, on its way from London to Portsmouth, by the axletree breaking. The accident occurred on a level piece of ground, to which the coachman going that road have given the name of the "Fair Mile." There were four inside and twelve outside passengers, of whom nine were convicts from Norwich, chained together by handcuffs and leg irons, besides the coachman and guard.
> The inside passengers escaped without injury, but were terribly frightened when the coach fell. The coachman was stunned by the fall, and received serious bruises on the temple; one of the keepers in charge of the convicts received very serious injuries - three of his ribs were fractured and he had met with other hurts.

> None of the convicts were at all injured. After some delay a van was procured, in which the convicts were conveyed to Portsmouth. The passengers also proceeded on their journey soon afterwards in another coach. The wounded keeper was left at an inn in the neighbourhood, and we have since heard that he is going on as favourably as can be expected. (Feb 1830)

In addition, robberies by highwaymen were not uncommon and the following articles appearing in the *Hampshire Telegraph* describe some incidents on the Portsmouth to London road:

> We hear that there is diligent search making after the Foot-pad who robbed the Portsmouth Stage Coach on Thursday who was seen last in the morning, at break of day, just by the house of Abraham Shard Esq, in Kennington Lane, as mentioned in our last. He was in a house coat, with a jockey's cap and was seen in St George's-Fields coming into Town soon after he had committed the robbery. (Feb 1742)

> As Mr Crowcher, of Portsmouth, was coming to town yesterday in a post-chaise, he was stopped about a quarter past six o'clock in the evening on Putney Common by a highwayman, very well mounted on a switch tail bay mare, who robbed him of his money, but said he did not want watches; he appeared in great agitation, and swore that he would either be killed that night, or have what he wanted. (1774)

> On Wednesday evening, about half past six o'clock, the Portsmouth diligence coming to town was robbed by a single highwayman within a mile and a half of Vauxhall turnpike; he took from the passengers three guineas and a watch and some silver. He behaved very politely to the passengers; but on the coachman's calling out to stop the highwayman, he turned back and fired his pistol at him. (February 1780)

> The Portsmouth coach was attacked between seven and eight o'clock on Thursday evening by three foot pads near the gibbet on Wimbledon Common.
> One of them, supposing an outside passenger to be the guard, snapped his pistol at him, which fortunately missed fire. He prepared to repeat it, exclaiming, "You're the guard, damn you," but, on the persons assuring him he was not, he desisted. His companions in the meantime robbed the inside passengers, five in number.
> This transaction occupied ten minutes at least, and by the time it was concluded a waggon came up, (the driver of which they desired to drive on). (Nov 1830)

The advent of the railways led to the gradual ending of coach travel and the following article in the *Hampshire Telegraph* in 1842, written by a Portsmouth coachman described how he had seen the introduction and demise of coach travel during his lifetime:

> I have lived to see the Portsmouth mail coach put on, and I have lived to see it taken off. Except one coach, I have lived to see all the London coaches put on, and it seems as if I should live to see them all taken off; although at one time there were ten up and ten down every day, and one three times a week. These coaches, if only half filled, must have taken 176 passengers every 24 hours, to and from Portsmouth.

> The one coach, when I was a boy, was two days and one night on the road; it went to Guildford the first day, where the passengers slept for the night, and went into London the next day. The turnpikes were not then finished.
> The mail was brought by a man or a boy on horseback. I brought it from Petersfield and got into Portsmouth at two in the afternoon.

> After that a diligence was put on that carried three passengers, and sometimes went empty. Then Mr Palmer put the mail coach on that carried four, prior to which the only way of travelling was on a horse with a guide - the guide went to bring the horse back.
> As for going on foot "'twas not safe as there were so many foot-pads about"; and there was not a public house between Halfway House and Mousehill that had five or six saddle horses ready for passengers to ride on the way to and from London and Portsmouth.

After the roads were made good, it was thought a great feat for a man riding with an express to go up to London and back in a long summer day; now it is to be done in nine hours.
Oh! These rail roads! - Besides having ruined the road, what will the farmers do with their hay, oats and straw?

The advent of the railways certainly revolutionised travel throughout the country, but in addition local travel was also changing with the introduction of bus services.

Trams and buses on Point.

Public transport in Portsmouth is first recorded in the form of a horse drawn bus service that was introduced circa 1840 between Southsea and North End, probably by the Portsea Island Conveyance Company. [47] By 1857 a further horse service was running to Old Portsmouth.

In 1863 the Landport and Southsea Tramways Bill allowed the Landport and Southsea Tramways Company to commence the first street tramways, which has resulted in an urban service being in service ever since. Under this Act, the first route to be constructed was from the Station Approach of Landport Station to Southsea (Clarence) Pier, at which point the tramway ran right on to the pier deck. The objective of this route was a quick transfer of traffic, both passengers and goods, to and from the Isle of Wight.

These single deck trams were drawn by two horses and officially commenced in May 1863. Two luggage trucks were hooked on to the passenger car and the track was of a gauge 4ft 73/4 ins. [48]

The Provincial Company was registered in 1872 as a holding company and a third subsidiary was formed in 1873 in the form of the Portsmouth Street Tramways Company which opened a route from the Floating Bridge (Broad Street) to North End in 1874.

An early horse drawn tram at the junction of High Street and Broad Street on its way to the Floating Bridge c.1885. © Portsmouth Museum Service.

122

Records show that an employee named Mr Steel started with the company in 1874 and was employed until his retirement in 1924 after 50 years of service. It is said that he went out with the first car at 8.30am and continued on duty until the last car went in at 10.30pm – an act of quite some dedication! At this time, there were only 8 cars on the road, 4 painted yellow and 4 painted green.

The yellow cars were stabled at North End whist the green cars were stabled on Point (Broad Street) [48]

The tram stable yard in Broad Street was situated near the *Blue Posts Hotel* on the west side of the road on the corner of Tower Alley, and the old yard remained with the rails still intact for many years until the marine artist W. L. Wyllie converted the building into his artist's studio in the early twentieth century, ripping out the cobble stones and tram tracks. When it was used to house the trams the rails led in from the Floating Bridge direction.

It is alleged that Wyllie purchased the site because it was rumoured it was to be sold for use as a petrol tank storage area or for a furniture store. This site location can still clearly be seen today since an entrance arch, which was constructed over the original doorway by Wyllie's chauffeur remained intact after wartime bombing. It was constructed with the latitude and longitude set into it and it is still maintained to this day, remaining clearly visible even though it has been slightly relocated.

The black and white photo shows the old site of the tram shed after demolition, and the colour photo shows a view today of the arch (repositioned) with its geographical coordinates.

Tram conductors had to provide their own uniform caps and were responsible for the cleanliness of their own car, in all aspects other than sweeping out and polishing the windows. The drivers were responsible for getting out and harnessing their horses and for oiling up the car's axle journal boxes. Initially the fares charged on the horse drawn vehicles began at a 1d minimum, rising by 1d stages to 4d. [49] In 1875 the penny fares on the Street Tramway were abolished and increased.

The route was still expanding throughout the city and excessive speed and frequency of service was regulated to run at a maximum frequency of once every half an hour.

Further routes were introduced, and by 1878 Portsmouth Point was included on the route of the Portsmouth Street Tramways Company with the one horse single decked tram cars being painted yellow and red.

In 1882 summer services started in late March, running every 7 ½ minutes from the Floating Bridge to Commercial Road, and to North End every 15 minutes. A direct service was also in operation to South Parade Pier.

In 1882 there were four separate companies in the Portsmouth area, all owned and controlled by the Provincial Tramways Company Limited. Therefore a Parliamentary Bill was promoted to amalgamate them all under the title of The Portsmouth Street Tramways Company.

By 1892 the horse tramway consisted of 58 tram cars, 249 horses and approximately 14 miles of routes. On December 31st 1900 the entire tramways undertaking of the Portsmouth Street Tramways Company was handed over to the Portsmouth Corporation.

The Corporation then converted the system from horse power to electric and a separate power station was built in Vivash Road for the trams. By September 1901 most of the electrification of the old tram system had been completed.

Early twentieth century photo at the Point near the Floating Bridge terminal during a very high tide with part of the carriageway flooded.

A view in Broad Street in 1916 looking north showing a tram parked up waiting for passengers. On the left hand side is a queue of traffic waiting to board the Floating Bridge ferry to Gosport.

In 1926 the Vivash Road power station was closed, and was replaced by the Corporation electric light power station in Gunwharf Road.

In 1930 there were two alternative routes operating from the Point and there are records of trams occasionally running into the water at Point.

By 1934 trolley buses, which were electric buses drawing electricity from overhead wires using spring loaded trolley poles, were running to and from the Floating Bridge at the Point. The terminal in Broad Street was unique to the city as it employed a reverser so that trolley buses reversed into East Street. [47]

This trolley bus route was abandoned in 1951 and the trolley buses were replaced with motor buses. By 1957 there were three separate routes operating from the Point.

When the Floating Bridge ceased its operations in 1959 this had a drastic effect on demand for the bus services to and from Broad Street, and the relocation of the Isle of Wight car ferry to the other side of the Camber in 1982 also reduced demand. Today there is still a regular bus service running to and from Spice Island but the frequency of buses is a shadow of the past.

However, perhaps this will change in the future due to the likely popularity of the new Land Rover BAR headquarters, together with the improvements planned for the historical arches nearby. Parking is very limited in the area, and with the likely increase in visitors, further public transport may be required.

Chapter 10

The Camber

In the twelfth century, Portsmouth was a small town situated in the south west corner of Portsea Island, adjacent to a small natural tidal inlet – an offshoot of the main harbour – called the Camber. This was an ideal sheltered inlet suitable for maritime activities, although development did not commence until the late fifteenth/early sixteenth century.

Development was recorded in 1514 when the Camber quay warehouses were built, in all likelihood to act as a victualling base for the King's Storehouse, and as a beer storehouse for the Brew House, since beer had previously been stored and buried in thatched trenches. [1]

> In 1538 Henry VIII built new defences for Portsmouth, as the west side of town had hitherto been undefended. Now it was entirely enclosed, extending the ramparts from the "Dock Bulwark" - the bastion at the north west corner of the town, to the Camber at Town Quay. Along the wharfs of Town Quay and the shore of the Camber, the line was formed by gabions, until they reached the Pales, palisade and gate across the neck of the Point. These works were completed in 1545. [10]

One of the earliest plans of Portsmouth (c.1545) shows development in the south east corner of the Camber, together with a Town Quay which is situated on the east side of the Camber directly opposite where East Street is today.

The Camber 1545 from Gates *Naval History of Portsmouth* © courtesy of *Portsmouth News*.

The famous Cowdray engraving depicting the sinking of the Mary Rose in 1545 shows much activity on the south east side of the Camber, but at that time the Point peninsula was undeveloped with the exception of the Round Tower.

During the reign of Elizabeth I, the next phase of works were undertaken under the direction of Richard Popinjay, government surveyor. These works commenced circa 1560 under his supervision and by 1579 the gabions along the edge of the Camber were replaced by stone walls, as was the palisade fence that cut off Portsmouth Point, which was supplemented with a strong gate flanked by two demi-bastions. [9]

The wall from the Dock Bulwark to the Camber Quay was also rebuilt in 1563 by Popinjay and a map dated 1568 shows that the town quay had a small dock in its centre and the quay had three cranes on it. The map also shows that the small dock in the quay had been filled in and the wharfage extended, measuring 163 feet by 50 feet. Popinjay's estimate for repairs to the quay, cranes and brewhouses was submitted in June 1563 and the works completed by 1568. [9]

Extracts from records possessed by the Municipal Corporation of Portsmouth and published by Robert East, record numerous grants and leases for land bordering the Camber between the mid-sixteenth and early seventeenth centuries outside Point gate on Point, and also inside the town near the gate

Some of these extracts for "Beach Land Granted and Demised" are reproduced below and indicate the first development on the Point bordering the Camber, although the first extract refers to land more generally within the town boundary:

> To Richard Newes, dated 12th December 1569:"A grant in fee farm, under the yearly rent of four shillings, of: - A messuage, or tenement with the backside and appurtenances thereto, near the Water gate and the Queen Mary's bake house, called *the Swanne*, on the east part, and the Camber on the north; in length towards the Poynt three score feet and in breadth to the Camber 1x feet."

(The *Swanne* bakery was situated immediately south of the Point Gate in the town).

> To James Hatch, dated 28th September 1607: A Grant in Fee, under the yearly rent of 6 shillings, of "A piece of waste or void ground without the Point gate on the west side of the highway leading from the said town (of Portsmouth) towards the waterside, called the Poynt; and also one other piece of waste ground sometimes partly overflown with the sea, without the said gate on the East side of the highway in breadth from the highway unto the Camber sixty feet."

Another one of several leases granted on land at the Point bordering the Camber was the following:

> To Richard Elton. 15th December 1608: "A grant in Fee Farm, under the yearly rent of six shillings, of a waste piece of ground without the Point gate on the East side of the highway leading towards the Point, extending from the highway to the Camber bounded by a Storehouse lately built by Mark James on the north and upon a waste piece lately granted to James Hatch on the south."

All these grants and leases demonstrated that the land bordering the Camber was actively being developed at that time. Around 1670 the Camber Bastion was constructed in the Inner Camber as part of the town's fortifications, constraining further development and expansion of this part of the Camber. [10] The Camber moat to the sea was built in 1680s, effectively making the Point an island and was later filled in sometime between 1847 and 1850.

As development accelerated on the borders of the Camber, and Point became more and more prosperous, the population rapidly increased but sanitation did not keep pace with this progress. The following record dated 15th April 1703, taken from the Municipal Authority's extracts, demonstrates the extent of the pollution in the Camber:

Item, we doe present that the throwing of Bloude and ffilth which comes from the Queen's slauter house downe the slipe at Town Keye, and over the said Keye is a common nusance and a prejudice to her Majesty's Subjects coming to the said Keye with their ships and vessels. [11]

Another declaration made reference to vessels mooring up and effectively blocking off the Camber:

Item we present that the layeing and continueing of any ship or vessel in or nigh the Hard Way between the Poynt and the Towne Keye to lade or be unladen or otherwise for any longer time than is absolutely necessary is very prejudicial to her Majesty's Service and a manifest hindrance to the Publick Good and Welfare of this Towne. (14th October, 1703)

In 1782 the Corporation, as property owner, pledged to repair and extend the "Publick Quay and Wharf". Part of the mud flats in the Outer Camber were reclaimed in 1797 for the New Gunwharf, resulting in more sand being deposited on the Point so boats were unable to beach there at mid-tide or low water. [50] In 1799 Lindegren's wharf at the Point with a crane was said to be the largest in the Camber

William Burridge built the Baltic Wharf and tower in the Inner Camber in the early nineteenth century, which had a lookout posted there to observe vessels approaching Spithead in order to ensure that local traders didn't miss out on potential business. William Burridge was a naval agent for Portsmouth and a banker, but a series of unsuccessful business ventures resulted in his bankruptcy.

In the late eighteenth century, it is likely that ships of the East India Company and the Dutch East India Company would have regularly arrived in the Camber to stock up with provisions and have maintenance work carried out. Pigs and cattle were landed in the Camber in the late eighteenth century to be offloaded and taken to the slaughterhouse of the Victualling Board. Coal has been landed at the Camber for many years and records confirm the existence of many coal merchants in Portsmouth in the late eighteenth century, some of whom lived near the Camber. One of the jobs associated with the delivery of coal was that of a "coal meter" whose job was to measure the amount of coal landed and they were paid per ton landed by the coal merchants.

Camber Quay late nineteenth century showing how busy it used to be and at least nine carts can be seen collecting coal in the picture.

Unloading coal in the Camber.

In 1811 the Board of Ordnance constructed improved wharf facilities near Quay Gate and the whole was later transferred to the Victualling Board. The Customs subsequently bought the Victualling operation in the Camber in 1828 after it was transferred to Gosport, and a new Customs House was built on the site. [50]

A new military hospital was built on the site of the old Camber Bastion in 1833-34. At this time access to the Town Quay was via Quay Gate, and the quay was a dynamic place of business as most of the heavy goods being brought from other towns by sailing vessels were landed there. It was possible to cross the Camber at low water by a ford that had existed for hundreds of years to gain access to Broad Street through Smocke Alley (East Street).

An inventory for imports in 1836 highlights the importance of the Camber with the listing of goods that included grain; Irish butter; bacon; sugar; eggs; poultry; apples; oranges; lemons; nuts; herrings, salt fish; casks of beer; wine and spirits. Imports other than food included coal; stone; deals; candles; soap; tallow; tar; slate; cement and timber. [50]

Instead of allowing the Camber to be developed by a private company as a commercial port, as had provisionally been arranged in the previous year, in 1838 the Town Council resolved to undertake the work itself – this being the first indication of that Municipal spirit which has done so much for the development of the city. [46]

In July 1839 the Camber Improvement Bill, promoted by the Corporation, received the Royal Assent, and in September the Council accepted a tender of £16,105 for the works decided upon.

These works were completed and officially opened in June 1843 and included the deepening of the channel from the end of Point to the Customs House and Town Quay to the projecting part of East Street so as to enclose the Inner Camber, constituting a wet dock and surrounding it with wharves. A further proposal suggested the construction of a dry repairing dock with suitable wharf, workshops and stores in the triangular space in the Outer Camber between East Street and the end of Point behind Lindegren's Wharf. [5]
Construction work on this new dry dock commenced in 1860.

Camber Bridge

With the expansion of Portsea and Landport, a decision was made in the nineteenth century to construct a bridge across the Camber, making the journey to and from Point much easier, and allowing movement of materials to and from each side of the Camber. A swing bridge was constructed in 1842 at a cost of £1646 at the narrow point before entering the Inner Camber. This was just prior to the completion of the Inner Camber construction works, completed in 1843. The bridge was more than eighty feet in length, spanning a gap of fifty four feet and was in two halves which swung up and down to allow access. It was surfaced with three inch planking and had a nine and a half foot wide carriageway as well as footways. [51]

In 1860 it was noted that the bridge was a great success and had an immense flow of traffic including horses and carts and other livestock. In 1866 the bridge became known as the "Quay Gate Bridge" and, in order to control the opening and closing of the bridge, the post of "Camber Bridge Keeper" was created.

In 1879 the Committee defined the duties of Mr William Quinton, Harbour Boatswain, as being responsible for opening the bridge when required, assisting in berthing ships, taking a daily account of all vessels unloading or loading in the Camber, seeing that the urinals are flushed daily, attending to the weighbridge, giving out planks etc. The wages for this job amounted to twenty five shillings a week.

Camber bridge in 1883.

Over the years the bridge became a focal point for trouble as the following passages describe:

> In October 1848 the attention of the police was drawn to the nuisance committed by the boys and crew of the potato vessels in the Camber who are in the constant habit of throwing potatoes at the passengers on the bridge.

In January 1851 four boys were charged with pelting an agent's clerk with "sprate and scud" from the bridge as he passed underneath in a boat. [53]

In September 1854 two men were charged with assaulting the bridge keeper. He was opening the bridge when these two labourers from a collier knocked off his hat six times, hustled him and jumped down on him. All the while there was a crowd throwing stones and otherwise annoying the bridge keeper. Apparently these sort of disturbances were continually being created on the Town Quay. [51]

In 1879 the harbourmasters monthly report stated that two cogs were broken in the pinion and a tender of £37 from Vosper & Co. was accepted to carry out the works.

In late 1879 there was a tragedy on the bridge when a child was run over and killed on the roadway. Following this tragedy the Committee reminded the boatswain to keep the walkways clear at all times. [52]

In February 1889 a screw collier struck the east end of the bridge damaging the plates of the bridge and stonework foundations which resulted in the vessel becoming stuck until the tide rose. [51]

In June 1904 the dock engineer reported that the bridge had failed to close on three occasions when part of the ironwork failed and as a result of numerous problems, the Town Council decided to replace the Camber bridge as it was unable to take the increasing weights of vehicular traffic. It was finally closed to traffic in February 1905.

The Camber Bridge with the Cathedral in the background. This photo taken sometime near low water shows how shallow parts of the Camber were at low water as it has dried out on the right hand side.

In October 1906 a replacement Camber bridge was opened, and on its opening the Mayor and Mayoress, Sir George and Lady Couzens, drove across the bridge from East Street to the Customs House side. The new bridge was hailed as a vast improvement on the old. It was lifted by two motors to make the operation easier and it was twice the size of the one replaced. The bridge, of the bascule type, was operated on a cantilever principle, in the style of Tower Bridge in London. The bascules were raised into a perpendicular position absolutely clear of the waterway, and vessels proceeding to or from the Inner Camber are not impeded in the slightest, while on the bridge abutments are placed bollards. Iron Gates were placed at each end for closing the road when the bascules are raised. [54]

This bridge lasted less than twenty years and was finally removed in 1924 due to the increase of trade in and out of the Inner Camber. Its removal caused much inconvenience to the residents of Point, particularly those children attending the Old Town School in Gunwharf Road as they now had to walk there via Broad Street. However, with the reduction in the strategic importance of Point, in reality its loss was probably not that significant to many. [55]

In order to assist shipbuilding in the Camber, in 1844 a four hundred and fifty foot slipway was built and leased to Thomas White which was later added to, thereby producing a facility which could handle boats up to 800 tonnes.

On 27th September 1859 the foundation stone to the New Camber Dock was laid by the Mayor, the estimated cost being £22,000. A tender was let, and between 1860 and 1863 the construction of a dry dock between the Customs House and Gunwharf Barracks was undertaken. This dry dock, five hundred and forty feet in length, had a workshop, saw pits, steam pit, smith's shop, and pitch furnaces. The first vessel entered it in 1863. [50]

The Inner Camber around 1870 showing how densely populated the area was at that time. Numerous Men of War can be seen moored in Portsmouth harbour.

Further construction works were undertaken from 1874 to 1877 with an extension of the Inner Camber wharf. Later some additional quayside space was derived from the dismantling of Quay Gate and adjacent guardroom and military accommodation, following an acquisition in 1883 from the Board of Ordnance. [50]

The Camber suffered from a problem of siltation, resulting in the Council having to carry out dredging works to be able to accommodate vessels of a reasonable draft, so with expansion in mind, the Council purchased the Baltic Wharf in 1879.

Boats aground alongside the quay wall in the Inner Camber in the late nineteenth century.

Even with the vast improvement works being carried out by the Council, the space in the Camber was still extremely limited as geographically it was unable to expand. However, one trade that was expanding in the early twentieth century was that of coal importation – fuelled by the demand from a growing population and military and naval barracks – and a coal yard was opened at Fratton Station. [50]

This trade became very important and resulted in the demolition of some properties in East Street by the Corporation, following which Messrs Fraser and White installed a massive handling and storage plant adjacent to the quay with large coal bunkers and overhead gantries to offload seaborne coal from their colliers. This reinforced storage structure measured two hundred and forty feet in length by ninety seven feet wide and could contain fifteen thousand tons of coal.

Fraser & White's coal bunkers can clearly be seen in this picture together with the overhead gantries and *Bridge Tavern* pub in the centre.

Etching by Harold Wyllie showing the old boathouse in the Outer Camber at Point, early twentieth century.

The Power Station

The first power station was built between 1892 and 1894 in St Mary Street, near the Camber where coal could easily be imported for the boilers and sea water used to cool the engines. It was so successful that expansion soon followed, and by the outbreak of the First World War output had reached more than three thousand kilowatts.

Expansion continued between 1927 and 1929, and at the same time the Camber Dry Dock was opened for colliers to deliver coal right to the door of the station. Eventually two vessels were built, the "*Pompey Power*" and the "*Pompey Light*" to transport the coal.

The dry dock that was used by the *Pompey Power* and her sister ship for delivering coal to the Power Station and stockpiled reserves of coal can be clearly seen. © Portsmouth Museum Service.

134

As time progressed further expansion occurred, so that eventually the whole site between Gunwharf Road, St George's Barracks and Warblington Street was occupied and two three hundred foot high chimneys stood proud making it a recognisable landmark from miles around.

Portsmouth Power Station.

At its peak the Power Station contributed four hundred and seventy five million units to the National Grid and drew in excess of six million gallons of sea water per hour from the Camber for condensing purposes. However, as technology changed it was finally made redundant by the Central Electricity Generating Board, and in 1981 the chimneys were demolished, followed by the building itself in 1983, to be replaced by residential housing. [56]

It is amazing to consider what a huge iconic structure this was, having dominated the landscape for many years, only to suddenly disappear!

A Council report in 1928 indicated that there were ten berths in the Camber accommodating vessels of up to just over twelve hundred tons and the available depth of water varied between a maximum of sixteen feet at high water springs and 4 feet at low water spring tides. The report also confirmed the number of cranes that were available for use, some private and some municipal, and the availability of silos and grabs, together with four large warehouses for storing general goods and a modern weighbridge up to twenty tons.

At this time there were five daily cargo services between the Camber and the Isle of Wight, and Coast Lines Ltd had a regular service of steamers with cargoes from Liverpool and other ports. Since 1925 the trade of the port had greatly increased, the principal imports being, coal, cement, tiles, bricks, stone, oil fuel, timber, potatoes, flour and onions, while scrap iron was the chief export. [5]

Fresh water, bunker coal and fuel oil were available at the Camber and the trading reported to the Council that year was most satisfactory and showed an increase on the previous year.

Vosper & Co, a local shipbuilding firm, had three slipways with a patent hydraulic slip to heave up vessels to four hundred tons, and in 1946 the Council agreed to construct a new one thousand ton capacity slipway, which was subsequently built to expand facilities. [57]

In the 1950s large colliers were still berthing alongside, bringing coal from the north east. Dutch and French boats brought cargoes of vegetables and fruit and Channel Island potatoes were unloaded in the spring each year. Barges arrived from the Isle of Wight landing crates and barrels of beer, and there were modern storage sheds, coal bunkers and travelling cranes spanning overhead, together with harbour offices and Customs buildings.

A typical scene c.1940 showing the Fraser & White coal silos and overhead gantries for unloading.

The Inner Camber.

Onion Johnnies

For many years the "French Onion Johnnies" were a regular sight around the Camber in the spring and summer, wearing their distinctive berets and striped tops, when they were taking their stocks of onions from the boats in the Camber and transporting to their warehouses locally, where they would splice them together and hang them on the handle bars of their bicycles before heading out to sell them locally. They were Roscoff onions and renowned for their quality and mild, sweet flavour.

The onion trade with the United Kingdom began in 1828, and a century later there were fifteen hundred sellers throughout the UK. I certainly remember them in the 1960s in Old Portsmouth and recall my father buying onions from a seller named Louis.

A couple of French Onion Johnnies transporting their onions on their bikes.

In 1960 a new slipway and car parking terminal was built behind Broad Street as a replacement Isle of Wight car ferry facility replacing the slipway and offices at the northern end of Broad Street. This work in the Camber was carried out in the area previously known by locals as "Dirty Corner", which was a tidal area with moorings and a foreshore where boats were laid up on the beach behind the old properties fronting the east side of Broad Street.

The Boathouse with the *Star & Garter* adjacent c.1959 with Point car ferry slipway beyond on the right.

In 1982 the current Isle of Wight car ferry terminal at Gunwharf Road on the east side of the Camber was opened, having been constructed on the site of the old dry dock and adjacent land.

With the advent of bigger steam powered ships, the physical restrictions of Camber Dock meant that it was bypassed for the larger capacity of the more recently developed Portsmouth Harbour, and commercial traffic began to diminish, moving north to Flathouse and Albert Johnson Quays instead.

The Camber is the home of the local fishing fleet, which still remains today, together with the adjacent dockside development of the commercial fish market. It also has a shore side dry stack facility and associated small firms, an expanding civil engineering maritime company and visiting berths for non-commercial craft.

As mentioned in Chapter One of this book, in 2014-2015 a very large building was constructed on the Town Quay as headquarters for Land Rover BAR to try and mount a successful campaign to wrest the America's Cup from the U.S.A in 2017. The lead up regattas have already started and an event was staged in Portsmouth in July 2015, successfully won by the Land Rover BAR team.

The old Town Quay sheds before demolition.

The new Land Rover BAR headquarters.

A Second World War bomb excavated during construction caused some minor delay to the project.

The Land Rover BAR boat with other competitors in July 2015 leaving Portsmouth harbour.

Chapter 11

Boat Building

With Portsmouth being a maritime port, it is no surprise that boat building has played an important role in the Point's rich marine history.

Although the predominant ship building activity in Portsmouth has been undertaken by the Royal Dockyard, there has always been boat building in the Camber area on the edge of the Point peninsula. As people were granted leases on land bordering the Camber from the beginning of the seventeenth century, so wharves were constructed and boat building soon followed.

Although detailed records are hard to find for the types and sizes of vessels built in the seventeenth and eighteenth centuries, more information exists for the nineteenth century, although it is thought that mainly smaller vessels – many of 30 tons or less, were built in the Camber during this time.

In 1833 an advert appeared in the *Hampshire Telegraph* for interested parties to purchase a shipwright's yard with storehouses and living accommodation that was registered in East Street, but fronted on to the Camber. This yard was described as waterside premises, confirming that premises for boat building were in existence at this time.

A little later in 1849 an "eligible ship building yard" was advertised for sale, following a bankruptcy, that was sited adjacent to the new Point Barracks in Broad Street facing Fort Blockhouse and described as possessing the capability of hauling up two vessels of 100 tons burden. This suggests that the yard launched their boats directly into the sea somewhere near the existing sally port near to where the old Vospers Social club was sited.

This photo c.1864 clearly shows shipbuilding being carried out in the Inner Camber and the yard is presumably that of Thomas White.

In order to assist shipbuilding in the Camber, a 450ft slipway was built and leased to Thomas White in 1844 which was later added to, thereby producing a facility to be able to handle boats up to 800 tonnes.

This was later increased to 3000 tons. White developed a patent for a slipway and exported this new slipway design but he later became bankrupt, although his son set up a ship building base in Cowes which became very famous. [50]

In 1886 John Read leased a slipway from the Council and later extended the lease. He is listed as being based in the Camber until 1912 and he registered one vessel that he built in Portsmouth at 125 tons.

Records show that boats registered in Portsmouth in the second half of the nineteenth century tended to be on a relatively small scale. Some of these were sailing vessels registering between 9 and 125 tons, and some were steam ships, again of a relatively small size. [50]

The most famous ship building firm associated with the Camber was Vosper & Co, which was established in 1871 by Herbert E. Vosper, who was only 21 years old at the time, near the Baltic Wharf in the Camber, later moving to a new site next to White Hart Lane and Broad Street.

Vosper & Co. initially built boats for the local fishing and whaling industries. Soon, though, the company was also building commercial shipping vessels, tugboats, and barges. They also developed their own engines, winning a reputation for its paraffin-driven engines at the beginning of the 20th century. The company also adapted its engines to other fuel types, such as steam and crude oil.
The period leading up to and including World War I gave Vosper a boost, and during this time it also turned its production toward support for the British war effort, producing work boats, dinghies, and tenders.

R.S.S Discovery in Camber dry dock. In 1925.

R.S.S Discovery in dry dock after refitting much of the hull. © Dundee Heritage Trust.

The end of hostilities naturally slowed new ship orders. However, a major project for Vosper after the war was the refitting of the famous *R. S. S. Discovery* in the old Camber dry dock in 1925. She had previously been used by Captain Scott on his explorations of Antarctica.

The *Discovery* was practically rebuilt for a whaling expedition and research work in South Georgia and other Southern seas and she set sail in October 1925. The refitting was an intricate job requiring special greenheart and oak to be brought in from abroad to renew the keel, keelson, sternpost and timbers at a reported cost of £114,000.

After Herbert Vosper retired in 1919, the company began to shift its direction toward building up its design and engineering operations, particularly to develop new engine designs. [58]

Vosper & Co.'s fortunes changed when Commander Peter Du Cane became managing director in 1931 and they then concentrated on high speed craft, including yachts, tenders and racing boats.

The company's V8 engine quickly became a driving force behind a new growth period for Vosper, and they became an important supplier to the Royal Navy, adding such ship designs as seaplane tenders to their repertoire. Vosper also helped develop a new class of motor-torpedo boat (MTB), capable of speeds of up to 48 knots.

This photo shows an entrance into Vosper & Co.'s yard in Broad Street in 1935 between old shops and residences near the old Blue Posts pub.

During World War II itself, Vosper produced hundreds of MTBs, gaining international renown while also developing new types of rescue craft, but the end of the war forced the company to once again turn to commercial construction to fill in the gaps left by the decrease in military orders.

Photo c.1939 of MTBs berthed at the Vosper yard in the Inner Camber.

During the 1950s, Vosper began developing a new class of air-sea rescue ship, the Brave Class series, capable of reaching speeds of more than 50 knots.

The death of John E. Thornycroft in 1960 precipitated the merger between Thornycroft of Southampton and Vosper. By then, both companies were enjoying strong international sales, each in their own specialized areas. With Thornycroft covering large-scale ships and Vosper supplying world-class patrol boats, the combined Vosper Thornycroft Holding PLC, created in 1966, became one of the world's leading shipbuilders. Throughout the end of the decade and into the next, international orders became particularly strong for the company, arriving from the Middle East and Asia, as well as from Africa. [58]

During these years it was quite normal to see fast patrol boats in the Camber being built and fitted out for navies around the world, particularly for the Middle East and Africa, and I recall seeing a couple of corvettes being built here in the early 1970s for Nigeria and Ghana. These boats displaced 650 tons when fully laden.

An excellent aerial view of the Camber c.1960 clearly showing Vosper & Co.'s yard with a large boat under construction and two fast patrol boats berthed alongside their quay.

A Frigate constructed for a foreign navy, demonstrates what a tight squeeze it was manoeuvring from the Vosper shipyard in the Inner to the Outer Camber with the assistance of the local watermen firm of J. Butcher & Sons Ltd. © Portsmouth Museum Service.

Building of smaller timber boats took place in the Camber and on Point at the end of the nineteenth and throughout the twentieth centuries. There were a number of different yards that existed throughout the years.

One of the earliest yards was that of John Dawson Feltham which was located in Bath Square, fronting on to the harbour entrance, next to the Customs watch house and was based there building yachts between 1888 and 1912, before his death in 1917.

The yard of John Dawson Feltham north of the Customs Watch House c.1900.

John Dawson Feltham was born in 1847 on the Isle of Wight and later married there in 1871. He may have worked in boatbuilding at Cowes before moving to Gosport where he was living in 1881 at North Street, then moving again to College Street Portsea sometime c.1887. He is first recorded as operating a boatyard in Bath Square in 1888, where he lived with his wife and seven children. Two of these children were named George and Harry Feltham.

John Dawson Feltham.

Men and boys outside J. D. Feltham's boat building yard c.1883. John Dawson Feltham is in the centre of the picture and the yacht in the background is the *Bird of Freedom,* a small yacht, but it is uncertain where this photo was taken. *Bird of Freedom* was very successfully raced in 1883 by Mr Popham, a member of the Royal Portsmouth Corinthian Yacht Club that was formed in 1880, following an inaugural meeting at the Prince of Wales Club, High Street, Old Portsmouth.

The next boat builder to establish himself on Point was A W. Clemens, and his yard was located in the north west corner of the Inner Camber with his address recorded as 48-50 Broad Street. He was known as a builder of wooden boats and resided here from 1903 to 1951. He built many yachts including the local *Victory* class which are the 20 ft. black clinker yachts regularly raced in the Solent, and I personally recall a lovely *Harrison Butler* designed yacht, named *Sabrina,* he built for a Portsmouth Sailing Club member. He also built several pilot launches that were used locally.

Drawing by Martin Snape (1853-1930) of Clemens boatbuilding yard in the Inner Camber.

The other two boat builders on Point at this time were brothers, namely George and Harry Feltham who were two of John Dawson Feltham's children who set up rival boat building operations in Broad Street near the beginning of the twentieth century.

George A Feltham born in 1881 first established himself at 11 Broad Street and then moved to 4 Broad Street in 1918 where he continued until 1975 in a house and boatshed with slipway into the Camber, that still exist today. His business card below shows that he started the firm in 1900.

George Andrew Feltham's workshop at 11 Broad Street. He is standing second from the right.

George Feltham's business card.

Brass plaque from one of his boats.

The size of the timber boats he built were constrained by the size of the premises and his grandson, Keith Feltham, recalls much work being done for the Admiralty during the Second World War, with numerous 27 ft. double ended "whalers" being built as ship's lifeboats. These boats could be rowed and sailed and after the war a new design of double skin construction was developed with an inboard engine. [59]

Whaler in the loft at 4 Broad
Street where the wherry
Sportsman was built.

Rob Roy under construction.

George also built the occasional larger boat up to 32 ft in length, one of which was the famous *Rob Roy* which was sailed across the Atlantic Ocean. On her return passage broke the record for the fastest single handed crossing in a yacht in a time of 21 days. She was built in 1956 and Keith Feltham recalls there were two others constructed in the 1950s of the same design, but with different rigs.

He also designed and built the Stormalong dinghy (length 12ft 6 ins. + short bowsprit) that was raced locally by members of the Portsmouth Sailing Club, and also built some 4 oared clinker rowing galleys.

One of George's designs which is still regularly sailed today is the *Sea View One Design*, a 12 ft. clinker dinghy based and raced at Seaview on the Isle of Wight. In the summer it is not unusual to see a fleet of more than a hundred dinghies at the annual regatta with their different coloured sails making it a real spectacle. This fleet must be one of the largest one design fleet of dinghies in the world based at a yacht club.

Certainly, his boats have lasted well, as it is still not unusual to come across a wooden clinker dinghy with his nameplate on the stern.

The 1967 Register of Yachts lists 12 yachts built by George during the years 1929 -1961 which varied from between 5 and 12 tons displacement.

Both George and Harry built South Coast Beach Punts as fishing boats on the south coast, and these boats had an inboard engine and were gaff rigged, often sporting dark tan sails.

During his youth, George was an accomplished oarsman winning the Portsmouth Harbour Sculling Championship and he built the famous local wherry, *Sportsman*.

George in his later years sitting on a boat near his yard in the Inner Camber.

After being in business for many years with his son working alongside, George passed away in 1975 and the firm G. A. Feltham & Sons sadly came to an end.

Harry Feltham, born in 1885, initially lived at 43 Broad Street for 16 years, and then moved to 27A Broad Street in 1930 where his premises extended through from Broad Street into West Street.

He built numerous cruising yachts including several 33 ft Mcgruer Class 8 tonners and similar sized yachts, and in 1953 he built a 25 ft carvel Chinese junk rigged Folkboat with unstayed mast named *Jester*, which became famous.

The owner who commissioned and designed her was a well-known war hero named Lieutenant Col "Blondie" Hasler (a former Royal Marine Commando). He had her built to participate in the first OSTAR single handed transatlantic race in which he competed several times.

Another famous yacht built by Harry was *Driac II* (32 ft), commissioned in 1932 for W. G. H. MacPherson, who sailed her around the world on his epic voyages. He was an outstanding collector of maritime art and his collection later became the basis of the National Collection at Greenwich Museum. He was also a Commodore of the Portsmouth Sailing Club.

Jester

Driac II

Harry and Stan Feltham together outside their premises in Bath Square with a newly launched yacht sometime in the 1950s.

Harry was another local boat builder who built boats for the *Victory* Class which was formed in 1934. In the 1967 Register of yachts there are 58 yachts registered as having been built by him between 1928 -1965 (of tonnage between 4 and 14 tons), although his nephew Stan built some of the later ones following Harry's death.

Living next door to Harry Feltham and Stan was a real experience, hearing the construction work going on, and after several months a new boat would be craned out or hauled out on a trolley into Bath Square, which was always a joy to behold!

A new boat being craned out from the West Street premises.

Harry Feltham in his loft.

I recall once reading a story about Harry agreeing to tow away a dilapidated vessel, which was the Club Ship of Fareham Sailing and Motor Boat Club in 1945. Apparently she had been badly vandalised and was in a poor state. Harry towed her away and she was broken up and burnt on VE Day 7th May 1945!

Harry had a reputation as being a good helmsman and was not averse to a bit of gamesmanship. He regularly raced in the *Victory* Class and passed away whilst racing one during an evening race in 1958.

Following Harry's death, his nephew Stan Feltham continued to run the business for many years until closing down sometime in the 1980s bringing boatbuilding to a close on Point.

The only boat builder still in existence in the area today is John Perry whose workshop is located on the east side of the Camber in French Street. John served a 5 year apprenticeship with Harry Feltham starting in 1949, together with four or five other apprentices.

John's standard of workmanship is renowned as being superb and during his career to date he has built 2 "Vertues", several "Victory" class yachts, "Folkboats" and an "X" class yacht, together with numerous other yachts, including his largest commission, a 32 ft. yacht.

He has had boatyards at Cosham, Wicor (Fareham) and Southsea before moving to his current location many years ago, at which point he took over the site from a locally famous marine engineer named Sid Thatcher.

John's most famous commission was probably that to build an 18 ft. sailing gig which was donated by Portsmouth to Sydney, Australia, as part of the bicentennial celebrations in 1987. The photo shows the replica gig in Portsmouth Guildhall Square at the handing over ceremony. I recall the boat so clearly, as she was one of the finest examples of boatbuilding that I have ever seen and a beauty to behold!

She was a full size replica of the gig used by Captain Arthur Phillip when he landed at Sydney in 1788 as part of the *First Fleet*, and was beautifully finished. I remember the civic celebrations held in the Guildhall Square at the time when the red carpet was laid out and the Queen and Prince Philip attended at the official handover.

The gig sailing in Langstone harbour in 1987. Image courtesy John Perry.

John is still in business today and remains the last of the traditional boat builders in the Point area.

John in his workshop July 2014.

Chapter 12

The Jewish Population on Point

The following quotation is an interesting description of how Point Jews were perceived by some:

> The Point was also famous for the dwellings of those kind hearted children of Israel who supplied the wants of the seamen at the moderate interest of about 500 per cent. Talk of your London Jews – keen as they are, a Point Jew would have cheated a dozen of them in an hour. [5]

There is sufficient evidence to indicate a community of Jews in Portsmouth prior to the 1740s. Portsmouth City Records show that in 1716 there were 5 public houses in Oyster Street, where Jews seem to have constituted the largest number of domiciles at that time and one of these pubs may have provided the public room in which a Jewish congregation could gather for prayer.

Jews of German and Polish origin came to work for shop keepers in coastal ports and were sent inland to peddle boxes of trinkets, laces, cigars and other portable goods to farmers, with similar services being offered to sailors on board ship. This Jewish pedlar presence seems to have commenced in Portsmouth in the 1730s.

White's Row in Portsea was where the first large congregation of Jews occurred and a synagogue was constructed in 1742 although there may have been an earlier synagogue in Oyster Street.

In September 1791, Robert Bell, editor of the *Weekly Dispatch* visited Portsmouth and wrote an article entitled "Excursion to Spithead" that was a journal of his visit. One of his excursions ashore was reported as follows:

> Went ashore after breakfast with the Major to Portsmouth, then to Portsmouth Common (modern Portsea), a place where some years ago there were no inhabitants and now there are a number of streets and 1200 inhabitants, of which one quarter are Jews. There are 3 elegant churches, called chapels of ease and 3 Jewish Synagogues.

This would suggest that at the end of the eighteenth century there was a thriving population of Jews living in Portsea.

Several Jews are known to have lived on Point in the early eighteenth century, thriving on the spending power of sailors from ships engaged in the war with France. [66]

In an *Interesting History of Portsmouth 1801*, J. C. Mottley observed that:

The Jews having considerable privileges in this town, have so far availed themselves of such a favourable opportunity as to occupy houses and shops in the first style of mercantile consequence in the above trades, whilst Christian artisans who are not so wealthy are obliged to content themselves with sheds, hulks, or any other similar place which can afford them a chance of supporting themselves by a traffic limited in proportion to the small extent of their little capital.

The local "Point Jews" were regular visitors to ships anchored in Spithead that were paying off and the following tales are stories associated with this trade:

William Robinson's "Jack Nastyface, Memoirs of a Seaman" published in 1836 describes the period 1805 to 1811, during which:

After the ships of the fleet anchored at Spithead, having returned home from a tour of duty, the Admiralty Commissioners came aboard bringing the money to pay the ship's crew, with the exception of 6 months pay, which by a government rule was held back from each man.

Robinson wrote that:

Perhaps only 1 in 20 men knows what he will receive, nor does the amount seem to matter particularly, and the men hurry down to their respective berths to their several ladies and then turn their thoughts to the Jew pedlars who have come aboard at the same times as the ladies, and they are ranged around the decks and on the hatchway gratings.
They are furnished with every article that will rig out a sailor, never omitting, a fine large watch and appendages, all warranted, and with which many an honest tar has been taken in; they can supply them likewise with fashionable rings and trinkets for their ladies, of pure gold, oh! Nothing can be purer! Yet with all Mordecai's asseverations, its purity may be doubted.

Jack recalls one occasion on a ship where one of the crew recognises a Jew aboard who has previously sold him and a number of his crewmates, a silver watch for five guineas that proved to be defective.

His messmates persuaded him to go to the Jew and bargain for a jacket, waistcoat and trousers and when he was wearing the clothes another crewmate was to act as boatswains mate and came up behind his crewmate with a ropes end and began to hit him driving him below calling him a skulking rascal.
The Jew expected the man to return, and at the end of the day he complained to the Captain who said he would punish the man if brought before him, but after searching below he could not find the man who had so ingeniously taken his revenge and possessed himself of a suit of clothes.
Mortified to think he should be so done, he swore, by Moses and the Prophets he would find the villain but he finally had to leave the ship amidst the grins and jeers of the whole crew who were much diverted and pleased to think that any of their shipmates had tact enough to retaliate so nicely on a Jew.

This suggests that Jews were not always very popular with some sailors and the following newspaper article written in 1783 confirms this view:

A person who goes by the name of Joey the Jew, a son of Israel, who kept a house of ill fame, had amassed a large sum of money by attending ships when they are paid off, selling tars a parcel of trinkets, heard that a ship was paying off and approached the Purser of this ship. Joey showed him an elegant gold watch for which he wanted 25 guineas and the Purser offered him 10 guineas which was refused, so he then had it valued by other reputable tradesmen who thought its worth to be 20 guineas.

The Purser then told Joey that his ship was to be paid off the next day and if he would let him have the watch for 10 guineas he would let him have "one side" of the ship (a phrase for letting those leeches rob one half of the crew)

The Jew interpreted the promise in that manner and let him have the watch for 10 guineas.

The next day Joey came alongside with his boxes and hailed the ship and started to ascend, when the Purser appeared and told him if he attempted to board he should "have the engine played on him"

Joey remonstrated that he had been deceived, but the Purser answered coolly saying to Joey "I promised you one side of the ship, I have kept my word, you have one side.

In 1758 a dreadful accident occurred to some Jewish traders when returning from a ship anchored at Spithead and was reported as follows:

Friday last the following accident happened off Spithead. His Majesty's ship *Lancaster* being paid that day, amongst the trades people that carried goods on board were a great many Jews who had large quantities of valuable effects with them.

The Jews not meeting with the success they desired were resolved to go ashore.

It blew very hard and they had a sailing boat which they hired for that purpose; about 20 Jews and a few other people got into the boat with all their effects, but they had not got far from the ship when by gybing the sail they were overset.

The ship's boats were immediately put off and took up nine or ten of them. There were nine Jews drowned and two died after they were brought on board and all the Jews boxes and effects were lost.

The memory of the Portsmouth Jewry was epitomised in Thomas Rowlandson's 1814 engraving of *Portsmouth Point* depicting the moneylender *Moses Levy*.

Portsmouth Jews, so folk memory would have it, were little more than low life insurers cheating *Honest Jack* out of his hard earned prize money and wages. The reality was often very different! [67]

Thomas Rowlandson's 1814 engraving of *Portsmouth Point* © National Maritime Museum, Greenwich, London.

Although some Jews cheated sailors of their hard earned money, as the years passed by numerous Jews gave great service to Portsmouth strengthening the local community. However significant the local Jewish population may have been in the life of Portsmouth, its size has never been substantial, but it can be said that service and charity stand out as hallmarks of Jewish presence in the city throughout their period of settlement.

Chapter 13

Smuggling Activities and the Customs and Excise Service

Customs duties on imported goods, such as wine, and exported goods, such as wool were well known as long ago as the year 1215 and had been in existence for many years before this, without raising hostility. However, taxes known as Excise payable on goods made in this country (such as beer and candles) were introduced during the Civil War (1642-7) to pay for Cromwell's Army and were much despised.

Smuggling was not a great problem to the revenue authorities until the late seventeenth century. Until this time, smuggling had mainly been of wool – known as "owling" - as there had been a duty on the export of wool since the Plantagenet times before the export of wool was made illegal in 1614. This smuggling was punishable by death, so smugglers became very well armed. [60]

In 1671 Charles II created the Board of Customs, an official body responsible for the collection of customs duties and in the 1680s Revenue Officers were provided with customs cutters to enable them to patrol the coast to catch smugglers.

After 1688 with the country at war with France, much taxation was levied on tea and spirits to help finance the war. These duties now made it profitable to smuggle, aided by the advent of the fore and aft rig on sailing ships, which meant they were much faster and more manoeuvrable.

By the end of the seventeenth century smuggling was big business. The revenue men often came off worst as the smugglers were very well organised, both afloat and ashore.

The area around Portsmouth was particularly suited to the illicit trade: - the Isle of Wight was especially vulnerable and the inlets and creeks of Langstone harbour, Chichester harbour and the Lymington and Beaulieu creeks were also ideal sites for smuggling.

By 1691 Portsmouth had become a port in its own right and the Customs Office had a Collector and Controller, Surveyor, two Waiters, Chief boatman, three boatmen, as well as personnel to deal with Gosport, Fareham and Emsworth. [60]

Customs officers had a range of responsibilities at this time including dealing with the revenues from cargoes, enforcement of quarantine laws, protection of wrecks, enforcement of navigation laws, registration of British ships, collection of light dues, control of emigration and immigration and enforcement of numerous prohibitions of goods.

The job of a Quarantine Officer was a very important one and if an officer allowed any ships, persons or goods to escape from quarantine, he was liable to the death penalty.

The prevention of smuggling was linked to activities in the adjoining harbours of Southampton and Cowes, particularly operations at sea in which the Service's cutters and cruisers were involved.

Portsmouth's geographical position made it the centre of operations, superior to both Southampton and Cowes.

It is unsurprising that the smugglers were able to ply their trade for so long with scant regard for the revenue men as the Customs service was undermanned and their relationship with the navy was not always the best. Indeed the navy had something of a reputation of indulging in a little smuggling on their own account and the searching of the effects of senior officers and the seizing of their goods by the customs officers was a source of irritation.

In the early part of the seventeenth century it was left to the Collectors to negotiate for the hire of boats for revenue purposes, although these vessels were greatly inferior to the smugglers vessels in their sailing ability and armaments.

Smuggling became a very serious business in the first part of the eighteenth century, and numerous revenue men were killed in the course of their duties. However, the tide turned somewhat in a case where seven smugglers were tried at Chichester in 1749 for killing a revenue officer. As they were all involved in the smuggling together, the judge found them all guilty and they were all hanged at the gallows, with five of them being hung afterwards at prominent places for all passers-by to see.

A great deal of time was spent by revenue officers at Portsmouth keeping an eye on naval personnel evading paying any duty on contraband which was split amongst the naval ratings. Much of the trouble was caused by the ships' officers neglecting to obtain permission before they moved goods on which duty was payable.

A case in point was that of the future Admiral Kempenfelt when he wrote from the ship "*Elizabeth*" in February 1757:

> Gentlemen, I beg leave to acquaint you that being appointed Captain of His Majesty's Ship the "*Elizabeth*" designed for the East Indies, I sent my things from the "*Lightening*", which I commanded before by water to the "*Elizabeth*" at Portsmouth where the officers of the Customs seized about 11 gallons of rum and 16 of port wine, which indeed was all the liquor I had. As it had been customary for the officers removed from one ship to another to be permitted to carry their liquor, I hope gentlemen you will grant me the same indulgence, which I shall esteem a favour and am etc. [60]

There were instances of ship's masters blatantly lying to customs officials and the following account from the eighteenth century could be said to push the boundaries:

> A Customs official boarded a 70 ton cutter called the "*Molly*" at Portsmouth. On inspecting the spirit room he discovered a hogsheads of gin containing 62 gallons which the captain said was for the crew of 16. The Customs officer then inquired if there was more liquor aboard and was told there was not. On searching the cabin, the captain admitted there was a small cask, picked up at sea, and this contained three gallons of brandy which had probably been four gallons. The captain said there was no more aboard, but the Customs officer continued his search and

discovered a locker which was opened and found to contain two new liquor cases, each containing twelve bottles of brandy, making in all eight gallons and two stone bottles of brandy containing five gallons.

Again the captain insisted there was no more but a further search revealed another twelve bottles of wine in a locked locker in the captain's cabin.

It would be difficult to find a more blatant example of deliberate lying and it demonstrates how unreliable it was to accept a captain's word when they behaved like this.

In Portsmouth harbour the long standing large naval presence would initially seem to discourage smuggling, but this was not the case as smuggling simply took on a different guise within the navy itself. Naturally the large organised classic runs ashore were prevented, but the contraband came in through semi legitimate means instead, as the personal property of the crews on the naval vessels and the East Indiamen. The East India Company's ships were usually escorted to Spithead where they lay at anchor, often with an insufficient Customs presence on board to protect the cargo. The convoys of East Indiamen brought in huge cargoes of tea and lay off at Spithead. There were usually half a dozen officers stationed on each merchantman to ensure that no tea was sold over the side to the small smuggling boats which tried to come out to them. This, of course meant that the Customs Service had insufficient men to carry out other duties. The monitoring of tea smuggling was evidently ineffective, for Customs records of 1764 show that ships of the East India Company smuggled tea into Britain at an estimated annual value of seven million pounds. [61]

The system was not perfect, and abuse often occurred, particularly in the guise of corruption. Corruption was no doubt as rife in Portsmouth as it was in other harbours, as Customs officials had many other duties to perform besides policing smuggling, as there were a large number of vessels that passed through the port. [62]

During the period in which smuggling was rife in Britain, Portsmouth was very heavily involved. Although Portsmouth was not suitable for large shoreline landings such as occurred elsewhere along the coasts, in sheltered coves and backwaters to both the east and west, there were nevertheless large quantities of goods smuggled in through the port.

It is easy to imagine the considerable amount of smuggled goods finding their way to Point with the large number of ships arriving from foreign ports around the world. Although much of this contraband probably came ashore in small loads, collectively it would have been significant and there must have been a steady trade in all the pubs, taverns and boarding houses.

Collecting payable dues for appropriate cargoes and carrying out searches to police the smuggling activity was a very difficult task, when one considers the limited number of staff available, the numerous areas of responsibility and the large numbers of ships that had to be cleared by Customs on a regular basis.

With regards the returning East India Company vessels, it was commonplace for some of these ships to be met off the coast before arriving at port, in order to offload smuggled goods into smaller boats that were landed at small isolated locations where there was little chance of being discovered by any revenue officers.

Unlike many other ports to the east and west, there are relatively few first-hand accounts of smuggling being reported in Portsmouth on its southern coastline due to the heavy Customs and naval presence. However, the Isle of Wight and both Langstone and Chichester harbours were well known for smuggling.

Throughout the years smugglers had refined the art of hiding goods and of avoiding duties on their imported goods, and a few of the methods adopted are described below:

Tea cases were fitted between the vessel's timbers and were made to resemble the floors of the ship.
18 lbs. of tea could be hidden under the cape or petticoat trouser worn by the fishermen and pilots of the vessels.

This sketch below indicates one method of how tea could be secreted on the body to bring ashore to avoid paying any duty.

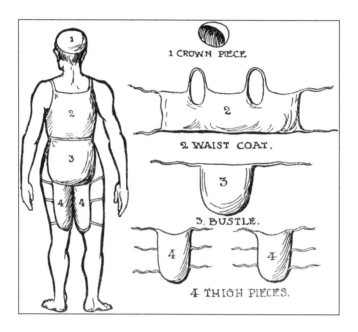

(1) Indicates a cotton bag which was made to fit the crown of a hat and herein could be carried 2 lbs. of tea. As the hat was worn when coming ashore, probably a sou'wester, there would be nothing suspicious in that.
(2) Cotton stays or a waistcoat tied round the body. This waistcoat was fitted with plenty of pockets to hold as much as possible.
(3) This was a bustle for the lower part of the body and tied on with strings.
(4) These were thigh-pieces also tied round and worn underneath the trousers. When all these concealments were filled the man had on his person as much as 30 lbs. of tea, so that he came ashore and smuggled with impunity.

Tobacco, another taxed commodity, was valuable contraband. Made into ropes of two strands, it was coiled with real rope in the luggers coming ashore, and was even put into a special compartment in casks of imported bones which were used for manufacturing glue.

The wooden fenders slung over the sides of a ship were also hollowed out and filled with tobacco.

Spirits, both brandy and gin, had intriguing journeys into our ports.

Brandy was chiefly imported from France. Excellent cognac was shipped from Roscoff. Gin, popular with the troops who had taken part in the Dutch wars, was imported from the Low Countries and Flushing in Holland exported gin chiefly to the East Coast.

Brandy or gin tubs, roped singly or in pairs and anchored with sinking stones, could be cut off easily and left with markers if Revenue Cutters were in sight. Tubs of spirits were packed into the hollowed keels of boats, hidden under false bottoms, or fitted into rafts or punts which were floated on a flood tide to persons waiting on the shore.

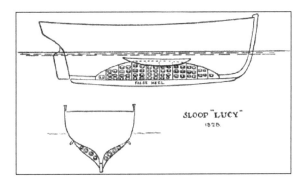

Sometimes kegs of spirits were secreted beneath hulls under their bottoms in a thin casing. They could not be accessed from inside the vessel, so to retrieve the contraband the boat would have to be beached. This method consisted of filling up the hollow area below the turn in the bilge, but it would have slowed the boat down when underway.

Barrels could be slung together and tied to a sunken rope with an anchor tied at each end and to retrieve the contraband a grapnel was used. Obviously these were dropped in well-marked locations that could easily be found later.

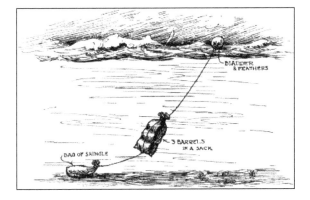

The method of smuggling in the sketch above involves 3 barrels in the sack and a 30 lb bag of shingle acting as a sinker, and the inflated bladder kept the sack floating about one foot below the surface and a small bunch of feathers acted as the buoy.

In *Smuggling in Hampshire and Dorset- Portsmouth, Southampton and the East Hampshire Coast,* John Smith tells of an eighteenth century attempt by smugglers to foil detection, stating that:

Towards the end of the 18th century the Portsmouth Customs Officers were being stretched to their limits by the daring exploits of smugglers and found it very difficult to patrol effectively. In 1783 a Customs boat was lying in wait for a rowing boat that was due to make a run ashore near Eastney Fort. However since the Customs vessel was sighted by the smugglers shore party, they set fire to the gorse and thus warned the smugglers who beat a hasty retreat. The Customs boat could not keep pace with the ten oared smugglers boat so they turned back and after landing at Eastney caught a single smuggler. There was a repeat performance the following night and the Customs caught more of the smugglers on the shore. A few days later the Customs were tipped off that a load was coming ashore near Fort Cumberland. Watch was kept by land and water and eventually over 60 smugglers turned up, disguised in masks and blackened faces, all armed with clubs and cutlasses. As soldiers arrived the smugglers fled but several were captured but these received light sentences because fever had broken out in the local prison.

Women assisted smugglers as signallers and carriers of messages, and also brought goods ashore. They used their voluminous skirts to conceal them, particularly in the case of silk, winding it round and round their bodies. There have been cases when they were found to have had their petticoats puffed out by bladders filled with spirits.

A report from the *Hampshire Chronicle* on March 25th 1799 stated that:

A woman of the name Maclane, residing at Gosport, accustomed to supply the crew of *Queen Charlotte* with slops, went out in a wherry to Spithead when a sudden squall coming on, the boat sank; the watermen were drowned but the life of the woman was providentially saved, by being buoyed up with a quantity of bladders, which had been secreted round her for the purpose of smuggling liquor into the ship, until she was picked up by the boat of a transport lying near. [63]

Caricature sketch by Rowlandson entitled *"Rigging out a smuggler"* © National Maritime Museum, Greenwich, London. The sketch shows a woman with contraband goods such as cognac, tea and perfume, having taken her outer garments off.

On August 11th 1828 it was reported that a seizure was made on the Point of 41 pieces of silk, amounting to about 2500 yards, which had been conveyed from Cowes in a steam vessel. This was quite likely imported on board an East Indiaman.

Records of more smuggling activity was published in the *Hampshire Telegraph* on January 18th 1836 when it reported that 71 tubs of spirits and a boat were seized at the Sally Port by the Tide Surveyor of Portsmouth. None of the crew were found, they were doubtless gone to call for assistance to smuggle off the liquor. On the same morning, 35 tubs of spirits were crept up on the Horse Sand by the *"Ferret"*, Custom House cutter; and several others drifted on Southsea beach, having been broken up by the late severe gales. This demonstrates that smugglers often left barrels of contraband spirits anchored beneath the surface and these were sometimes blown ashore in heavy weather.

In May 1849 the Commanders of both the Coast Guard Station at Southsea Castle and the Coast Guard Harbour Station noticed a steam tug vessel named the "*Royal Charter*" leaving the harbour without the usual lights. They suspected all was not well and waited for the vessels return: when she did she had a boat in tow. They hailed her from their small boats to heave to, but she ignored them and ran for the harbour even though several musket shots were fired across her bow.

Once in the harbour the steamer was boarded and a number of men were arrested. A raft of tubs , which it appeared the steamer had been towing, was discovered, consisting of 150 tubs of treble proof pale brandy, each containing between three and four gallons. The captured men, including the captain and engineer, and the brandy, were conveyed to the Customs House and the magistrates men remanded them for a week when they were brought before a court and were convicted. Apparently the steamer had been taken without the consent of the owner. [64]

The original Customs House stood opposite the ancient Quay Gate in Oyster Street and then moved to the lower end of Broad Street into the old Ordnance store which was converted for the purpose. Subsequently a new large dark brick building containing all the requisite offices and stores was erected in 1785, having in the rear communications with the Camber. [78] The Customs watch tower overlooked the harbour from Bath Square and the Customs House in Bath Square is listed in 1755, but it was not until 1835 that a small pier was constructed adjoining the watch tower, but the existing pier and lookout was not constructed until 1905. The small boats of the revenue officers were kept here and a watch kept day and night. No vessel entered the port without being hailed and proper inquiries made.

View of the Customs Watch house slipway with the *Isle of Wight tavern* to the north.

In 1799 the Camber was the base for the larger Customs boats which then numbered three, two of which were 100 ton cutters, each with a crew of 24. The crew were armed and all vessels arriving from foreign lands were boarded and checked, although it is likely that collusion was commonplace.

Revenue cutter chasing a smuggler from original painting by Charles Dixon R.I.

In a list of '*Revenue & Excise Cutters*' published in 1805 there were two vessels listed as being stationed in Portsmouth, with jurisdiction of Portsmouth and the seas surrounding the Isle of Wight. These vessels were the "*Antelope*", which was 105 tons with a crew of 24 men, and the "*Roebuck*", which was 140 tons with a crew of 30 men. Other cutters were stationed adjacent to this area and covered the whole coastline where smuggling was a threat.

In 1819 the navy supplied 8 ships and 3 tenders to Portsmouth to assist in preventing smuggling. These ships would have already been in commission, and in some cases certain vessels were employed in the Preventative service for only part of the year.
Without the Revenue cutters the navy could not have dealt with all the smuggling activities, and this was explicitly admitted by the Admiralty in 1822.

In 1820 there were eleven Revenue cutters under the command of the Commander-in-Chief at Portsmouth. [65]

The properties built by the Board of Ordnance near Quay Gate in 1811 were transferred to the Victualling Board and then bought by the Customs authority in 1828.

A new Customs House was built on the site, making the Broad Street structure redundant.
H M Customs was strengthened in 1809 due to the increasing numbers of naval vessels and prize ships arriving in Portsmouth. Goods were inspected and dues paid and if smugglers were caught, their boats were sometimes impounded and sold off.

In 1798 the duty on Imports at the Custom House in Broad Street was £79,000, coast duties were £15,500 and export duties £2000. The duties on wine alone in the same year were £22,000 which was increased in the year 1815 to the huge sum of £137,912. [6]

Posters such as this were published in the eighteenth century to assist in catching smugglers.

A typical advert that appeared in the *Hampshire Telegraph* in February 1801 advertising an auction of previously seized contraband to be held at the Custom House.

ADVERTISEMENT.

On THURSDAY, February 26, 1801, at Ten o'Clock in the Forenoon, will be
EXPOSED TO PUBLIC SALE,

AT the CUSTOM-HOUSE, Portſmouth, the ſame having been ſeized and legally condemned,

Brandy	551	Gallons.
Rum	9	Bottles.
Geneva	1493	Gallons.
Wine	{ 60	Gallons.
	{ 6	Bottles.
Serges	2	Bales.
Compounds	11	Bottles
Woollen Cloth	60	Yards.
Lime Juice	4	Gallons.
Pictures	4	No.
Coffee	38	lbs.
Copper	600	cwt.
Oſtrich Feathers	300	No.

A WHERRY and Materials; alſo, ſome OLD CORD-AGE and STORES, from the Roebuck cutter.

☞ The Spirits for Private, Uſe.

May be viewed two days before the Sale, by applying to the Warehouſe-Keeper.

Other goods advertised for Public Sale at that time included whisky, sweetmeats, fans, red lead, ship's anchors, sugar, coals, salt, shawls, candles, chocolate, tea, anchovies, cranberries and spruce beer.

One interesting public sale held on 22nd February 1802 advertised approximately 450,000 Concale oysters.

CUSTOM-HOUSE, PORTSMOUTH.

On MONDAY, the 22d Day of February, 1802, at Eleven o' Clock in the Forenoon,

WILL BE EXPOSED TO PUBLIC SALE,

At the Cuftom-Houfe, Portfmouth,

ABOUT 450,000 CONCALE OYSTERS; the fame having been feized, are now to be Sold, being a perifhable Commodity.

The government sometimes placed advertisements in local publications across Britain offering a reward for information leading to prosecution and conviction of persons bribing or attempting to bribe employees in the Customs Service. The following advert appeared in the *Hampshire Telegraph* in December 1802:

CUSTOMHOUSE, LONDON,
December, 1802.

WHEREAS Advertifements have at different times appeared in the Newfpapers, offering Sums of Money for the procuring of Places or Situations in the Customs, inserted either by Perfons not aware of the ferious confequences which attach upon tranfactions of this nature, or by Perfons of a different defcription, with a view to delude the ignorant and unwary. The Commiffioners of His Majesty's Cuftoms think it neceffary to have it generally made known, that, in addition to the Punifhments which the common Law would inflict upon the offence of bribing or attempting to bribe any Perfon intrusted with the difpofal of any Office, the Statute paffed in the fifth and sixth years of the reign of King Edward the Sixth inflicts the penalty of Incapacity to hold fuch Office, in the Person purchasing, and the forfeiture of office in the Perfon felling : And that in case any such place or situation either, shall have been or shall hereafter be procured or obtained by such corrupt means ,they are determined to enforce the penalties of the Law, and to Profecute the Offenders with the utmost feverity. And they do hereby promise a Reward of

ONE HUNDRED POUNDS

To any Perfon or Perfons who will give information and fatisfactory proof of any place or situation in the Cuftoms being so obtained so that the Parties concerned therein may be proceeded against accordingly.

By Order of the Commiffioners,

JAMES HUME

The 1830 the *Pigot & Co Commercial Directory* for Portsmouth lists the Customs House as being located on the Town Quay. It also details the staff employed at that time, recording 97 staff including Collector, Comptroller, Landing Surveyor, Comptrolling surveyor and Jerquer, Warehouse keepers (2), Clerks (5), Searcher, Landing Waiters (2), Inspecting Commander of Coastguard, Tide surveyors (2), Quarantine Superintendent, Medical Superintendent, Commissioner of Pilots (3), Customs House Agents (7), Lockers (6), Tide Waiters (22, includes those in the out towns), and Pilots (40).

The Collector took the general superintendence of the Portsmouth office and the Comptroller acted as a check upon him.

The Landing Surveyor appointed and superintended the Landing Waiters.

The Landing Waiter kept an account of goods discharged from vessels arriving from foreign ports and superintended the landing and shipping of goods coastways. The Jerquer's duty was to examine and check the Landing Waiter's books. The Searchers took an account of goods to be exported to foreign parts. The Tide Surveyors superintended the Tide Waiters and boarded them on vessels arriving from foreign parts for the purpose of preventing any fraud on the revenue from being committed. They kept an account of goods as landed from vessels.

The Customs House Agent attended to the duty of passing the Customs entries of goods on their importation and exportation and transacting the relative business at the Custom-House, and also passed the entries required for the clearance of ships. The Locker was in charge of the bonded warehouse.

The considerable number of staff working for the Customs House indicates the extent of the work involved in inspecting ships leaving port and arriving from abroad, securing duties payable, and also being at the forefront to tackle the huge problem of smuggling.

In April 1833 the commissioners of the Customs Service placed an advert in the *Hampshire Telegraph* requesting sealed tenders for the disposal of their old building at the Point. The premises were described as being situated near the extremity of the Point and consisting of two very substantial and modern brick buildings. One of these was fronting the sea, and was about 60 feet by 40 feet and three stories high. The other building was in the rear and was about 65 feet by 30 feet, consisting of four stories of warehouses well-timbered and fit for immediate use with access to a crane from the water for vessels of light tonnage.

After the battle of Waterloo, the British government made a determined effort to put down smuggling by using the surplus navy ships, personnel and Coastguard, and a coastal blockade of the south east coast was established.

By the late 1820s the effectiveness of the two forces was apparent and in 1831 the Coastguard Service became responsible for the entire coastline and ultimately became the preventative force.

This measure drove smuggling underground, but primarily the gradual introduction of a free trade policy in the 1840s brought smuggling down to reasonable proportions by the middle of the nineteenth century.

Smuggling was still taking place, but it was more likely to be concealed on larger ships among the cargo in vessels trading to commercial ports.

The Customs House remained the biggest building in the Camber but the council had the foresight to acquire the building from the Office of Works in 1879, facilitating its demolition and the construction of a smaller building in 1885 to the east of the site, in order to provide more space between it and the swing bridge.

The Custom House and watchtower on the end of the pier still exist in Bath Square today, and were still in use in the 1980s before being closed and converted to a residential property.

Custom's Watch House pier in the mid twentieth century.

The Point and Camber area today are much quieter places, and the maritime trade from foreign ports has ceased, with those ships that still visit Portsmouth now being directed to the Commercial Port north of the Naval Base where the Customs House is located nearby.

At the height of the smuggling era, Point would have been a fascinating place to be with the diversity of goods coming ashore, both legally and illegally, from ships returning from foreign lands.

Chapter 14

Memorable Events Associated with Point

North Carolina Fleet

Throughout the years the Sally Port near King James's Gate has seen some famous comings and goings, with royalty arriving and leaving, Royal Naval personnel setting off and returning from voyages and battles, and a number of famous voyages of discovery and early settlers leaving from this famous spot on Point.

On 26th April 1587 a group of 91 men, 17 women and 9 children set sail from Spithead, having previously embarked from the Sally Port at Point, in three ships bound for Virginia in the New World, as the second colony under the command of John White.

This voyage was to establish the "Cittie of Raleigh" on the Chesapeake Bay where the natives were friendly and the area was suitable for deep water navigation. Raleigh wanted to establish a permanent North American settlement to harass Spanish shipping, mine for gold and silver, explore a passage to the Pacific and bring Christianity to the native inhabitants.

The previous first colony settlement in the New World was led by Sir Richard Grenville in 1585 who left more than 100 men on the island of Roanoke before returning to England for more supplies. The colonists had trouble with the local natives and struggled to survive through the winter with dwindling supplies.

These colonists later took the opportunity to return to England with Sir Francis Drake, who had unexpectedly stopped at the island following a raid on Spanish New World colonists further along the coast.

Two weeks after their departure Grenville arrived to a deserted island, but left 15 colonists with supplies to hold the position until reinforcements could be brought from England.

The first vessel of the Portsmouth fleet, the largest named the "*Lion*" under the pilotage of a Portuguese pilot named Simoon Fernandez, arrived at Roanoke on 22nd July 1587. After landing, none of the 15 colonists left previously on the island were to be seen, only the bones of one person. The fort had been razed to the ground but some of the houses remained in an overgrown condition.

White wished to leave and take the colonists elsewhere but Fernandez having unloaded the colonists, refused to allow them back on board for various reasons (possibly the real reason was that he wanted to return to the West Indies to plunder Spanish ships). He eventually left sometime in August after the three ships had been unloaded.

With the colonists ashore and prepared to make do until future supplies could be brought in, White subsequently set sail in one of the remaining two ships and left a small ship for the settlers with the intention that he would return with more supplies as soon as possible.

Unfortunately for White when he arrived back in England war had broken out with Spain and it was almost three years later in 1590 that he returned to Roanoke with further supplies for the colonists.

When White finally returned to Roanoke there was no sign of any of the 117 colonists, and all that was found was a carving on a tree. The word "CROATOAN" had been carved as three years earlier it had been agreed that if the colonists moved out they should indicate where they were going by a carving such as this.

However, following numerous searches during the following years the "Lost Colony", as it became known was never found. [68]

Charles II Marriage to Catherine of Braganza

In April 1662 Catherine of Braganza started out for England to marry Charles II but storms delayed her passage and she did not reach Portsmouth until May 14th. She landed at 4pm in the afternoon and although the King was not there to meet her, the nobility and gentry were present together with multitudes of Londoners. "And the Mayor and Aldermen and principal persons of the Corporation being in their gowns, and with a present and a speech ready to entertain her; the cannon and small shot both from around the town and the whole fleet echoed to one another the loud proclamations of their joy". [5]

The Corporation presented her with a salt cellar of crystal supported by four eagles and four greyhounds of silver gilt and driving through the principal streets of Portsmouth she retired to her apartments at the Domus Dei. Her landing is represented on the copy of an engraving below.

Catherine of Braganza landing on a raised causeway somewhere between the Round Tower and the present sally port. "Illustrated History of Portsmouth" W. G. Gates. Reproduced courtesy of The News Portsmouth.

The engraving shows courtiers bowing, coaches and horses waiting and bare headed troops with halberds in their hands lining the way to the gateway with a sort of portcullis to it near the old St James's Gate. The Royal Standard floats on the Magazine Tower (Square Tower) at the bottom of High Street and cannon and musketry are being discharged from the batteries and a considerable fleet is also gathered at Spithead.

The King arrived in Portsmouth on May 20th and after trying unsuccessfully to persuade Catherine to have a single Protestant wedding ceremony, it was agreed that she should be married twice as she wanted to have a Catholic ceremony.

On Thursday May 22nd she had her Catholic wedding in her bedroom with few persons present and the more public ceremony took place later in the day, though not as one might expect in the Domus Dei, but in the chamber of the Governor's house.

The King later wrote to his mother-in-law, the Queen of Portugal, saying "Being now freed from the dread of the sea and enjoying in this spring time, the company of my dearest wife, I am the happiest man in the world and the most enamoured, seeing at close hand the loveliness of her person and her virtues, not only those which your Majesty mentioned in your letter – simplicity, gentleness and prudence- but many others also. I wish to say that I cannot sufficiently either look at her or talk to her" [5].

Another letter containing the King's less complimentary first impressions of his wife is on display in the Royal Garrison Church.

The Register of the marriage is carefully preserved at St Thomas's Church.

Capture of the *Hermione* – Spanish Treasure Ship

Between 1500 and 1850 there was little other gold in Europe apart from that found in Spain. During this period there was a huge amount that flowed across the Atlantic. It has been estimated that between 1500 and 1820 there were 17,000 voyages of treasure ships from America to Spain carrying gold worth £4,000,000,000 sterling at sovereign value.

The only legal method to acquire any of this gold was to pick a quarrel with the Spanish Government and declare war. [79]

In 1744 the Spanish galleon the "*Nostra Signora de Cabadonga*" was captured and the "*Centurion*" brought her into Portsmouth Harbour with treasure which was landed and taken to London in 32 wagons.

It so happened that Britain declared war on Spain in 1762 and the Spanish treasure ship "*Hermione*", at sea off Cadiz, was swiftly captured by two British frigates, the "*Active*" and "*Favourite*", who later divided the prize money between them.

The treasure was brought back to Portsmouth and landed on Point beach and conveyed through the town under military escort with the ship's crews carrying the captured Spanish flags headed by bands of music with great crowds lining the streets.

The treasure which was at the time an all-time record in prize money was conveyed to London under escort to the Tower.

The division of prize money was regulated by an Act of 1708 which laid down the proportions into which the value of the prize was to be divided.

In general the full value of the prize, ship and cargo, went to the captors as follows: the captain had three eighths, of which he gave one to the flag officer under whom he served; the other officers down to Sergeant of Marines had three eighths, with the more senior officers having a bigger share; and the remaining two eighths went to the rest of the crew, again shared according to seniority. The Admiralty also paid £5 per head of the enemy crew at the commencement of the engagement to encourage captains to engage the enemy together with a bounty. {79]

The prize money of "*the Hermione*" was divided as follows:

THE *ACTIVE'S* SHARE

	£	s	d
To the Captain, Sir Richard Dacres	66,053	3	9
To three Commissioned officers at £13,004 14s 1d each	39,014	2	3
To eight Warrant officers at £4,336 3s 2d each	34,689	5	4
To twenty Petty officers at £1806 10s 10d each	36,130	17	8
To 150 seamen and marines at £485 5s 4d each	76,132	13	0
Total *ACTIVE'S* share	251,020	12	0

THE *FAVOURITE'S* SHARE

	£	s	d
To the Captain	64,872	13	9
To two Commissioned officers at £12,974 10s 9d each	25,949	1	6
To seven Warrant officers at £4,324 10s 11d each	30,273	8	5
To sixteen Petty officers at £1,802 0s 4d each	28,832	6	3
To 110 seamen and marines at £484 2s 5d each	53,253	14	4
Total *FAVOURITE'S* share	203,181	4	3

(Extracted from the Naval Chronicle)

By today's standards, this would probably have resulted in many of the crew becoming millionaires.

The "*Active*" being entitled to the whole of the bounty money, makes the difference in the Shares divided between the two ships.

One has to remember that in 1796 the pay per annum did not exceed £150 for a frigate captain, £75 for a lieutenant and £12 for an ordinary seaman, so this prize money would have enabled even the humblest seaman to set himself up in a cosy pub. [79]

The way the prize money was divided was considered very unfair by many, and the following nautical anecdote sums it up: a sailor, who previous to an engagement was seen by the lieutenant to be, as he thought hiding behind the gun. "You are funking, Sir" said the officer. "No, I am not" said the seaman, "I am praying". "Praying, Sir; what are you praying for?" enquired the officer. "Why, Sir, said the sailor, I'm praying that the enemy's bullets will be shared out like the prize money – that most will go to the officers".

This was one of the grievances that led to the Nore and Spithead mutinies, and the ordinary seamen summed it up as "guineas for officers; halfpence for seamen". [16]

The Nore and Spithead mutinies occurred in 1797 and happened as a result of discontent among the crew on lower decks. They were not violent insurrections, but more in the nature of strikes demanding better pay and conditions.

General Wolfe – The Landing of his Body at Point

General Wolfe was born for greatness and even at the young age of 20, six years after joining the army, exerted himself in so masterly a manner at the battle of Laffeldt that it drew the highest praise from the head of the British army.

He had distinguished himself at Rochefort and Louisberg, with both these expeditions having left from Portsmouth and he later returned in 1755 when he wrote an unfavourable account of his stay. He remarked on the lack of discipline he found with disorderly soldiers including dirty, drunken, insolent scoundrels made worse by the wicked nature of the place, where every kind of corruption is carried to excess. It was the lack of order and the evil conditions of the town, especially at Point, which struck Wolfe, as struck many other observers during the century. [69]

He was so appalled by their behaviour that he wrote the following to his mother:

> The necessity of living in the midst of the diabolical citizens of Portsmouth is a real and unavoidable calamity. It is a doubt to me if there is such another collection of demons upon the whole earth.

The famous expedition to Quebec was fitted out in Portsmouth Harbour and the fleet set off on February 17th 1759 to Canada where Wolfe ultimately defeated the French, in a victory that will forever denominate him as the conqueror of Canada.

However, on the 14th September 1759, aged 32 years old, when victory was in his grasp, Wolfe received wounds to his wrist and then to his chest. As his condition deteriorated he was given the news that the enemy were defeated and he then expired almost immediately.

His remains were placed in spirits and brought back to England and from the anchorage at Spithead on November 17th 1759 his body was lowered out of the ship into a twelve oared barge, towed by two twelve oared barges and attended by twelve others to Point beach.

Guns were fired from the ships at Spithead at minute intervals for a period of one hour.

The regiment of Invalids marched from the Parade to Point beach to receive his remains and at approximately 9 am the body was put into the hearse and proceeded through the garrison.

The escort, with flags at half mast, conducted the body to the Landport gate from which point the hearse and coach continued their journey to London. On 20th November Wolfe's remains were interred in the family vault at Greenwich and a monument erected in his memory in Westminster Abbey. [16]

The Birth of Australia

On 13th May 1787 a fleet of eleven ships under the command of Captain Arthur Phillip R.N. set sail from Spithead bound for Australia. Captain Phillip was to assume the role of Governor to a penal colony to be established somewhere on the recently charted coast of New South Wales.

The first fleet arrived at Sydney Cove on 26th January 1788, an event which is regarded as the birth of modern Australia.

The first place of arrival was Botany Bay but the area was deemed to be unsuitable for settlement due to its lack of water and open exposed anchorage so the fleet moved on to Port Jackson (Sydney)

This fleet consisted of six convict ships, namely the *"Alexander"*, *"Charlotte"*, *"Lady Penrhyn"*, *"Friendship"*, *"Prince of Wales"*, and *"Scarborough"* and five other ships:-- HMS *"Sirius"*, HMS *"Supply"*, the *"Fishburn"*, *"Borrowdale"*, and *"Golden Grove"*.

This first batch of unwilling colonists comprised 568 men and 191 women, all of whom apparently arrived in reasonably good health after a voyage of 252 days for most. The voyage encountered problems as some of the convicts on the *"Scarborough"* unsuccessfully attempted a mutiny. There were only 23 deaths on the voyage which was considered good in those days for a trip of such length.

The convicts, guilty of petty crimes that were the result of trying to survive the conditions of England at the time (such as stealing a loaf of bread) were the pioneers who through hard work and perseverance made the colony survive and expand to the stage of self-sufficiency from which Australia grew. [70]

By July 1788 all the ships had left with the exception of the naval vessels *"Sirius"* and *"Supply"*.

Although the settlers suffered many problems with lack of food in the early days, the future arrival of more ships carrying convicts and supplies enabled the colony to finally establish itself.

Between 1788 and 1850 England sent over 162,000 convicts to Australia in 806 ships but the first fleet of 11 ships whose occupants of convicts and marines left from the Point are today known as the "First Fleet" and acknowledged as the "Founders of Australia".

First Circumnavigation of Australia

On 18th July 1801 HM sloop *"Investigator"* set sail from her anchorage at Spithead, following their departure from Point, under the command of Commander Matthew Flinders, Royal Navy. Flinders was one of the most skilled navigators at that time following in the footsteps of Cook and Bligh. Indeed he sailed under Bligh's command on one voyage as a midshipman.

His commission was to circumnavigate and chart the then unknown continent of Terra Australis known as New Holland (in the west) and New South Wales (in the east).

He was well known for having identified and corrected the effect upon the magnetic compass readings of iron components in wooden ships, giving rise to the universal "Flinders bar".

His circumnavigation was carried out between 6th December 1801 and 9th June 1803. However due to being detained on Mauritius for more than six years on his return, he did not return to England until 24th October 1810.

In 1800 vast areas of Australia's coastline were still completely unknown. Dutch navigators had charted some and James Cook had charted the east coast in 1771, while Britain had established the first convict colony in modern day Sydney in 1788. Little was known of the coastline between, and virtually nothing about the interior of this huge continent.

After much of Flinders's survey was completed the "*Investigator*" was condemned in 1803 as she was badly leaking. He sailed as a passenger later on the "*Porpoise*" but she was lost on the Great Barrier Reef and eventually he set sail for England on a 29 ton schooner called the "*Cumberland*" with the intention of getting another vessel to complete his survey of Australia. However, he was captured by the French in Mauritius after he was forced to seek assistance there due to the poor condition of his ship.

After his arrival in England, it was some time before his full publications – giving an account of his travels - were completed, and when he died on 19th July 1814, it was the day after the book and atlas were finally published.

Flinders's book was widely read, and in 1824 the British Admiralty agreed that the newly charted continent should be officially known as Australia, as proposed by Flinders.

His name is now associated with more than 100 geographical features and places in Australia confirming how important his survey and mapping of Australia proved to be. [71]

Shocking Accident

"On 24th June 1809 on a bright sunny day the beach at Point was alive with bustle and excitement.

They were very busy at the crane on Lindegren's Wharf, for several hundred merchant men were waiting at the Mother bank, outside Portsmouth harbour, to be supplied with beef, pork, biscuit, flour and rum; there was also a quantity of casks and baggage left on the beach by the 2nd Battalion of the 8th Regiment, who a day or two before had landed from foreign service.

A party of soldiers were down early that morning assisting in the removal of the baggage. The youth of Point found ample amusement in staring at the tall sergeant discussing the height of his plume and the number of buttons on his gaiters. An old Irish woman, a soldier's wife, was washing near where the baggage lay on the beach when another soldier's wife who was smoking, asked her if she would take a whiff. She did, but finding the tobacco would not burn, she struck the bowl of the pipe against the pebbles, when a little of the tobacco fell out and set fire to a few grains of powder that were scattered on the beach. This flew to a crate and exploded some loose cartridges which then communicated it to a cask of powder.

An explosion followed that carried death and destruction around; many men were blown into the sea;- arms and legs flew over the roofs of houses in all directions and thirteen soldiers were known to have been blown to pieces; one man belonging to Captain Patton's boat had his legs broken and many others were beaten down and sadly maimed. People staggering to their doors in Bathing House Square saw a human body, minus arms and legs falling through the air which struck in front of the Customs Watch House and fell quivering to the ground. Another trunk was blown against the front of the *Union Tavern*, splashing the bedroom windows with blood. Bystanders, recovering slightly from the shock began taking some of the sufferers into the

Fortitude Tap, one of whom was a drummer boy - described by witnesses as a mere child, whose face was scorched beyond recognition and whose uniform was like a burnt blanket.

A few daring men, dreading that some of the casks scattered about might also contain gunpowder (which no doubt some of them did) at once rolled them into the water to prevent another catastrophe. Lindegren's stores were on fire and as it was supposed they also had gunpowder stored in them, people hurried through Point gates in great numbers. Sentries were placed at the gate to facilitate egress, but ingress was denied to all.

When the fire was subdued and the agitation had somewhat ceased it was found that the effects of the explosion had been very terrible. Houses were unroofed, window sashes and doors had been blown in and there was scarcely a whole pane of glass remaining on Point; arms, legs and other portions of human bodies were found on the roofs of the houses in all directions, and the ebb tide carried out the harbour that day a goodly quantity of hats, caps, clothes and portions of mutilated humanity.

It was never known the number of persons who were injured by the explosion, but it must have been very large and it is estimated that from thirty to forty lives were lost by this culpable negligence of some person or persons in authority.

It is curious to note that the woman who was the cause of the accident escaped uninjured after the first slight explosion took place, as she was endeavouring to make her escape when she was beaten down by the greater shock which followed; a large washing tub was blown upon her, nearly covering her body and to this circumstance she attributed her preservation." [16]

Dwarfs on Point – the Visit of "Tom Thumb"

In 1864 the world famous dwarf, Tom Thumb, his wife and travelling company came to Portsmouth. The procession passed down Lombard Street and across the Camber Quay.

Tom Thumb at his wedding in 1863.

His company had successfully appeared before the chief Royal families of Europe, and thanks to the talented advertisement of Barnum (the legendary American showman), the inhabitants of Portsmouth flocked to see this unique show.

Tom Thumb was originally christened as Charles Stratton in Bridgeport, Connecticut in the USA in 1832 and when he died in 1883 he was 31 inches in height.

His carriage, said to be 20 inches in height was painted blue and white, picked out with gold and was drawn by Shetland ponies, and the coachman and footmen were boys dressed in medieval costumes.

On that day Old Portsmouth was full of visitors and the Broad Street tradesmen and Bath Square merchants were prosperous. [4]

The Collision of the Paddle steamer "Duchess of Kent"

On the afternoon of 3rd September 1909 the steamer *'Duchess of Kent'* collided with a vessel named the *'Transporter'* outside Portsmouth harbour.

The *'Transporter'* (2000 tons) left her berth in Portsmouth harbour at about 3pm on a strong ebb tide. At the harbour entrance she was going at half speed and noticed the *'Duchess of Kent'* rounding by Fort Blockhouse and heading towards the harbour entrance. The *'Transporter's'* pilot immediately took evasive action and also gave two blasts on the siren to indicate that he was moving to port. There was no reply from the passenger steamer and eventually they collided as the *'Transporter'* struck the steamer on her port side tearing a large hole into which the sea poured.

Fortunately the captain of the *'Transporter'* did not reverse, otherwise the steamer would have sunk quickly, with a likely loss of life but the huge cargo boat held her bows in the cavity to keep the smaller vessel afloat and gradually pushed her towards the shore to the south of the Sally Port and Victoria Pier where she grounded. This only took a few minutes and then the *'Transporter'* returned to the harbour.

As soon as the collision was witnessed the dockyard sent two tugs to assist but on arriving at the scene, neither were required.

A passenger on the *'Duchess of Kent'* later told a reporter that at the time of the collision the ship was full of passengers (400 in total). On the force of the collision they were thrown on the deck but quickly recovered and the crew acted admirably, reassuring the passengers, when they saw that the vessel was badly damaged.

Very soon cutters and boats were alongside and the women and children were shipped as soon as possible to the shore, the men and crew following. As far as could be seen there were only minor injuries

Large crowds watched with interest as the event unfolded and later the curious spectators, numbering three or four hundred, covered the fortification wall of the Saluting Battery. Many more viewed the vessel from Victoria Pier where the gash in the vessel's side could be seen, giving a clear idea of the narrow escape she had, given how much more severe the outcome might have been, particularly if she had been struck in deep water and the weather conditions had been less favourable.

The work of salvaging the damaged steamer began the next day by a party of workmen from the Railway Company's Works, Southampton. Temporary repairs were carried out to the hole in the vessel's side, installing planking across the aperture with a backing of concrete to make it watertight. She was then taken to Southampton for permanent repairs to be undertaken.

The *'Transporter'* was an unusual vessel as she was built for the purpose of transporting two submarines – which had been built by Vickers, Son and Maxim - to Japan. She had successfully undertaken this voyage before returning to the UK and was being used for conveying machinery to Portsmouth. At the time of the incident she was returning to Barrow. [8]

The *'Duchess of Kent'* aground near Victoria Pier showing the large gash in her port side.

The summing up of the formal investigation that followed the incident reported thus: "The Court found that the subsequent collision and consequent damage to the *'Duchess of Kent'* were caused primarily by the default of the Trinity House pilot of the *'Transporter'*, who in contravention of the Regulations for preventing Collisions at Sea did not keep to the starboard side of the fairway, and by his wrongful act in going to port instead of starboard when he first sighted the *'Duchess of Kent'*. The master of the *'Duchess of Kent'* is to blame for breaking the local regulations as to speed. It is to be added that after the impact everything possible was done by the pilot and master of the *'Transporter'* to minimise the results of the accident, and they gave material assistance in beaching the damaged ship. Their action and coolness and judgement of those on board the *'Duchess of Kent'* coupled with the steady behaviour of her passengers undoubtedly prevented the heavy loss of life which must otherwise have ensued." [72]

The Great Wherry Race

This article was written in October 1963 by John Feltham, the grandson of George Feltham, boat builder on Point.

Christmas Eve in the year 1919 started cold, grey and blustery at Point, Old Portsmouth. Before the conclusion of that day there would be a great triumph, a bitter disappointment and not a little bloodshed. A legend was destroyed, about £13,000 changed hands and an intriguing tale of Point boatmen was born.

It was the day that the Portsea wherry *'Flying Cloud'*, said to be unbeaten in 63 races, lost to the Point wherry *'Sportsman' that* had been built specially for the challenge. The six miles race, despite being held in fresh winds and a choppy sea, was won in a relatively short time. A veil of mystery seems to have fallen on the exact details of what happened before that final challenge, but one man remembers it perfectly – Mr George Feltham who built, and was an oarsman in the *'Sportsman'*.

Circumstances of the challenge.

Mr Feltham of 4, Broad Street, Old Portsmouth is 82 next month. His memory of the events of the day, however, is perfect and he remembers the circumstances of the challenge. *"'Flying Cloud'* was a boat of about 24 feet owned by Mr A. Grubb and was operated by the Portsea watermen. She was built before the beginning of the century and was said to have done 63 races unbeaten," he recalled.

"Just before World War 1, in 1913 I think, a 20 foot wherry built a year before by my father, John Feltham beat *'Flying Cloud'* double-handed in a regatta. This was the *'Bird of Freedom.'* She was not big enough for four oarsmen really, so both boats raced with only two. This is why *'Flying Cloud'* was beaten – she was bigger and heavier.

"After the war, my father challenged Mr Grub to a four handed race with the same boat for £25. We were boat beaten – everybody said so, it was a mistake to race her."

The outcome, however, was another challenge, this time from George Feltham himself. He bet Mr Grubb £25 that he could build a wherry to beat the legendary *'Flying Cloud.'*

The Building Inspection.

"I had a good laugh during the building," said Mr Feltham. "Mr Grubb said he and the crew would like to take a look at my boat in the loft. I agreed, as long as they did not pass any remarks. Well, before they came, I painted *'Sportsman'* green inside and a dark slate colour outside to make her look heavy."

"Then I bored two holes in the loft floor, fixed thin wires to the keel at the bow and the stern, ran the wires through the holes and hung half hundredweight pigs on them. Then I pushed a few shavings up close to the bow and stern." "When the deputation came in, they naturally wanted to lift her (Grandfather told me that at this point he deliberately busied himself at the bench and turned his back on them). I heard them muttering 'What a weight'." "After this, Mr Grubb told me that the men would not race unless the stakes went up from £25 to £100." "It was a joke really, because *'Flying Cloud'* was built of yellow pine and we of silver spruce. Anyhow, although £100 was a great deal of money to me, I finally agreed. One hundred pounds it was...."

Practice at nights

Mr Feltham had his first idea of how the race would go after a practice by lantern light one evening in November. *'Sportsman'* raced *'Bird of Freedom'*, the crews exchanging boats for the return trip. *'Sportsman'* went like a shot from the gun. Nobody knew about it but George Feltham, his brothers Fred and Harry, who had helped with the building, and a handful of Point watermen who could keep their peace. The crew that was to race on Christmas Eve was chosen a few days before, and had very few hours practice together. There were the Feltham brothers George, Fred and Harry and Charlie White, with Alec Cockreil on the helm. None of them weighed more than nine stone. This was their secret! *'Sportsman'* floated light and Harry Feltham, using a shorter oar than the others, could maintain a stroke to kill the average oarsman. By two o'clock on the afternoon of December 24th, Point was thick with people. Excitement was high and the bookies were shouting the odds. They were not favourable to the Felthams. Betting was two to one against them. "I would not tell anyone what I thought the result would be." Said Mr Feltham, "but I did not bet on the race. The £100 was enough, win or lose."

Colossal cheer

At 2.30 pm they were off, to a colossal cheer from the thousands of Christmas Eve watchers. Bets were still being made, money was being piled on money. The crowd had less than an hour to wait. In the boats the struggle was on. *'The Sportsman'* was being forced into the lead by the four light oarsmen, with the stroke handling a ten foot oar and the other oarsmen's eleven foot ash oars.

"There was a fresh northerly wind, and a bit of a bobble on. But we set out for the first mark, the King's yacht moored on number six harbour buoy, past the north corner of the Dockyard, at 36 strokes a minute. Nobody thought that we could keep up this pace, but we finished at 38."

"In rowing, you are half way there once you take the lead. We took it and never lost it again". The *'Flying Cloud'* and the *'Sportsman'* went up to the top of the harbour, down along the Gosport side (where there were thousands more watchers), and out of the harbour to number six fairway buoy. As *'Sportsman'* approached Point beach for the finish, with' *Flying Cloud'* still passing the Round Tower, Mr Feltham had a premonition of what might follow.

Disappointed People

"About £12,000 had changed hands, and a great deal of it had been lost. There were some really disappointed people in that crowd. I told the boys to get off Point as fast as they could and not come back." "They did, and people pressed money or curses on them as they went up Broad Street. I went home and locked the doors." "It was then that Point exploded. There must have been shock at first, then reaction. Fights broke out amongst the 'fors and againsts', there were near riots late into the night, many a head throbbed for days. The *'Flying Cloud'* legend had been split beyond repair by the size of her defeat and several persons had lost large sums of money. 'She was boat beaten,' said Mr Feltham. *'Sportsman'* was fast, *'Flying Cloud'* was living on laurels. Anyone could have built a boat to beat her if they had taken the trouble. It was just that no one expected to win and they were content always to come second. Also she usually had good crews."

….And after

'Sportsman' went on for many years and kept her reputation. She was a fast boat, a flyer!

As to the fate of *'Flying Cloud'*, Mr Feltham is not sure, but of one thing he is certain – she never raced in Portsmouth again – at Point, Portsea, Flathouse, Hardway …..

The Grounding of H.M.S Vanguard

On August 4th 1960 the last of the British battleships, *'HMS Vanguard'* left Portsmouth harbour under the tow of five tugs, heading to the breakers yard at Faslane Scotland. Nearing her fourteenth year of service, she had a displacement of 44,000 tons and had been stripped of most of her fineries.

She left her berth at 10am and had two tugs with bow lines, one on the port side, one on the starboard side and one astern and left with a rousing reception.

As she passed the Isle of Wight ferry jetty and the Gosport ferry pontoon she suddenly veered to starboard towards HMS Dolphin and following a series of frantic whistling and hailing, her course was altered to port. However, this had been over corrected and she moved to the other side of the harbour, heading towards the Point.

She was closing in fast on the *Still & West* public house and the Custom's House pier and warnings were given by the ship's crew to stand clear as there were hundreds of onlookers taking photos of her last voyage.

Vanguard slewed at 45 degrees and her bows stopped yards short of the Customs House pier and Pickford's quay after the quick thinking crew let go her starboard anchor which fouled the old Floating Bridge chains which luckily held. The tugs rallied around and were at "full astern" as she grounded in 24 feet of water on the ebb tide.

Tugs pulling frantically to try and tow *'H M S. Vanguard'* into deeper water.

As the tide was ebbing fast the situation became desperate, and as the anchor was cut loose, other dockyard tugs were ordered to the scene as there was a danger that the battleship's stern would slew and block the harbour. The harbour was temporarily closed to all shipping at this time.

The combined efforts of six dockyard tugs could not move her but the added power from the two ocean-going tugs that were to tow her to Faslane saved the day as she was pulled off at 11.15am and went on her way to Faslane. At a speed of 5 knots, the voyage was completed in a time of five and a half days without further incident. [73]

It was very dramatic at the time and I remember it well as a youngster with all the excitement generated on Point as the drama unfolded with the crowds building as the news spread.

It was joked by sailors who used to frequent the *Still & West* on a regular basis that *'HMS Vanguard'* had tried to call into the pub for her last G & T and a pint for the lads"

Funeral Procession of Michael Gaughan, IRA Hunger Striker

On Monday 3rd June 1974, Michael Gaughan, a 24 year old member of the IRA died whilst on hunger strike in Parkhurst prison on the Isle of Wight.

He had been sentenced to seven years imprisonment for his part in an IRA fundraising mission to rob a bank in Hornsey, North London, which yielded just £530 and for the possession of two revolvers. Initially imprisoned at Wormwood Scrubs, he was then transferred to the top security Albany prison and later taken into solitary confinement at Parkhurst prison.

Gaughan was demanding to be treated as a political prisoner and asked for a transfer to a prison in Northern Ireland. The authorities rejected his request so he wrote out a list of his demands and went on hunger strike, commencing on March 31st 1974. After his death following a 64 day hunger strike, members of the IRA arranged to take his body back to Ireland for the funeral.

Bodyguard units protecting all 21 members of the British Cabinet were strengthened and security precautions were tightened in case Irish extremists tried to retaliate for his death. [74]

There was very tight security on the Isle of Wight as the procession travelled from the hospital mortuary at Newport to Fishbourne, where they boarded the car ferry to Old Portsmouth.

On arrival at Portsmouth the hearse carrying the body came ashore from the car ferry at East Street to the sound of pipes played by the Irish piper, Larry O'Dowd, and it was escorted by approximately 50 men wearing the black berets of the IRA, some of whom acted as pall bearers.

Disembarking from the car ferry at Broad Street ©
courtesy of the *Portsmouth News*.

The body of the Irish martyr was draped with the flag which had covered Terence MacSwiney, Lord Mayor of Cork, who died on hunger strike in Brixton prison in 1920. The party of mourners travelled in the coach behind the hearse and I clearly recall seeing them as they moved along Broad Street at a very slow pace with the coffin covered in the Irish Republican tricolour. [75]

The body was taken to "lay in state" at the Sacred Heart of Jesus church in Kilburn, London, before being flown to Ireland.

Gaughan's funeral was held on June 9th 1974 in Ballina, County Mayo. It included a full republican burial with full military honours and was attended by over 50,000 people, making it larger than the funeral of former Irish president, Eamon de Valera.

Bibliography.

1. The Spirit of Portsmouth, A History. J. Webb, S. Quail, P. Haskell, R. Riley.
2. The condition of the children of the poor in mid-Victorian Portsmouth. Portsmouth Paper No 21. Mrs Jean Stanford and Professor A. Temple Patterson.
3. Portsmouth's water supply 1800-1860. Portsmouth Paper No 12. Mary Hallett, B Sc (Econ), M.Phil.
4. Reminiscences of Old Portsmouth. F. J. Proctor 1931.
5. Illustrated History of Portsmouth. William G. Gates 1900.
6. The History of Portsmouth. Lake Allen 1817.
7. Observations on the coasts of Hampshire, Sussex and Kent by the late William Gilpin, M.A. 1804.
8. The Hampshire Telegraph.
9. A Military Heritage – A History of Portsmouth and Portsea Town Fortifications. B. H. Patterson.
10. Fortifications in Old Portsmouth – a guide by Arthur Corney.
11. Extracts from the Records of the Municipal Corporation of the Borough of Portsmouth. Robert East 1891.
12. The Western Defences of Portsmouth Harbour 1400-1800. Portsmouth Paper No 30. G. H. Williams, CBE, MA.
13. The History of Portsmouth. Henry Slight.
14. History of Portsmouth – A Naval Chronology. William G Gates 1931.
15. Down Memory Lane, The Pubs of Portsmouth. Ron Brown.
16. Annals of Portsmouth. W. H. Saunders 1880.
17. Sir Frederick Madden's Hampshire newspaper clippings, Portsmouth Central Library.
18. The Hampshire Telegraph. January 8th 1816.
19. Notes on the Topography of Portsmouth. Alexander N. Y. Howell 1913.
20. The Hampshire Telegraph. February 13th 1847.
21. City of Portsmouth Records of the Corporation 1928, 1929, 1930. William G Gates.
22. Sporting Magazine, volume 27, October 1805.
23. Portsmouth Breweries 1492-1847. Portsmouth Paper No 51. Philip Eley.
24. The Pubs of Portsmouth from old photographs. Ron Brown.
25. Stephen Pomeroy (homepage.www.ntlworld.com).
26. We shall fight on the beaches: Defying Napoleon and Hitler, 1805 and 1940. Brian Lavery.
27. The Naval Chronicle. March 9th 1803.
28. The Naval Chronicle. September 1803.
29. www.Royalnavalmuseum.org.

30. The Hampshire Telegraph. March 9th 1818.
31. The Hampshire Telegraph. December 31st 1821.
32. Portsmouth and the East India Company in the Eighteenth century. Portsmouth Paper No 62. James. H. Thomas, B.A, PhD, F. R. Hist. S.
33. www.Britannica.com.
34. www.Historypolitics.com.
35. Offshore Ferry Services of England and Scotland: A useful guide to the Shipping Lines and Routes. Peter. C. Smith.
36. Old Sea Wings, Ways and Words, in the days of oak and hemp 1890. Robert C Leslie.
37. Brannon's Picture of the Isle of Wight 1855.
38. "Jack Nastyface, memoirs of a seaman". William Robinson.
39. Crossing the Harbour, the Portsmouth Harbour Story. Lesley Burton & Brian Musselwhite.
40. The Portsmouth Book of Days. John Sadden.
41. www.History.inportsmouth.co.uk.
42. The south west Maritime History Society –www. swmaritime.org.uk.
43. The Hampshire Telegraph. March 2nd 1840.
44. www.Wightlink.co.uk.
45. Portsmouth Guide books 1775, 1802, 1822, 1823, 1835.
46. City of Portsmouth Records of the Corporation 1835-1927. William G Gates.
47. Portsmouth Corporation Transport. Bob Lowe.
48. The Tramways of Portsmouth. S. E. Harrison.
49. Jubilee Booklet 1951.
50. The Camber 1565 – 1901 (draft) R. Riley.
51. www.myfamilymatters.org.uk.
52. www.movablebridges.org.uk.
53. The Hampshire Telegraph. October 1848.
54. The Hampshire Telegraph. 24th October 1906.
55. The News. September 9th 2000.
56. www.history.inportsmouth.co.uk (the Power Station).
57. City of Portsmouth Records of the Corporation 1946-1955. G E Barnett.
58. www.fundingunivers.com.
59. www.history.inportsmouth.co.uk (Boat building at Point by Keith Feltham).
60. Smugglers & Revenue Officers in the Portsmouth Area in the Eighteenth Century. Portsmouth Paper No 22. Edward Carson, MA, FIL.
61. Smuggling in Hants and Dorset.
62. www.smuggling.co.uk.
63. www.burtonbradstock.org.uk.
64. The Hampshire Telegraph. 15th May 1849.
65. The King's Cutters and Smugglers 1700-1855. E. Keble-Chatterton 1912.
66. Portsmouth Jewry. Portsmouth Paper No 41. Aubrey Weinberg.
67. www.thejc.com.
68. www.encyclopaediavirginia.org.
69. The Story of Portsmouth. Henry Sparks.
70. www.historyaustralia.org.au.
71. www.adb.anu.edu.au-Australian Dictionary of Biography.
72. Formal Investigation of "Duchess of Kent" collision October/November 1909.
73. www.battleshiphmsvanguard.homestead.com.

74. Herald-Journal. June 8th 1974.
75. Portsmouth News.
76. An Early Victorian Street, the High Street, Old Portsmouth. Portsmouth Paper No 26. John Webb, F. R. Hist. S.
77. The Industrial Archaeology of the Portsmouth Region – Portsmouth Paper No 48. R. C. Riley, B. Sc. (Econ), PhD.
78. Chronicles of Portsmouth. Henry Slight, Julian Slight. 1828.
79. The Frigates An account of the Lighter Warships of the Napoleonic Wars. James Henderson.
80. Kelly's Directories of Portsmouth.
81. The Demise of Demon Drink? Portsmouth Pubs 1900-1950. Portsmouth Paper No 58. Philip Eley and R. C. Riley.
82. Sadler's Hampshire Directory 1784.
83. The Borough, being a faithful, tho' humorous description of one of the strangest garrisons and sea port towns in Great Britain. Robert Wilkins 1748. .
84. The Hampshire Telegraph. November 1808.
85. The Sporting Magazine, volume 27 October 1805.
86. Portsmouth Breweries 1492-1847. Portsmouth Paper No 51. Philip Eley.

Lightning Source UK Ltd.
Milton Keynes UK
UKHW050949180419
341229UK00004B/7/P